THE GREAT LITTLE HOT DOG COOKBOOK

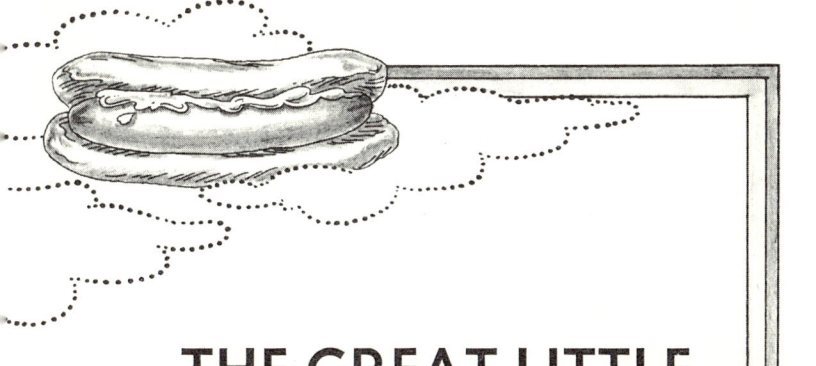

THE GREAT LITTLE HOT DOG COOKBOOK

John A. Gould

Illustrated by Ed Nuckolls

DOUBLEDAY & COMPANY, INC., Garden City, New York
1973

ISBN: 0-385-02441-X
Library of Congress Catalog Card Number 72-92212
Copyright © 1973 by John A. Gould
All Rights Reserved
Printed in the United States of America
9   8   7   6   5   4   3   2

to Jill,
who started this book,
and Nan,
who finished it.

Preface

As originally designed, this was to be a bachelor's cookbook, dedicated to the propositions that men need more help in the kitchen than women, and that the most nearly universal item in American refrigerators (bachelor or otherwise) is a package of hot dogs. I felt that single men needed and deserved a manual for the preparation of this important staple.

Lately, however, suggestions from friends and publishers have led me to the conclusion that perhaps certain female minority groups could benefit from a rebriefing on the hot dog question. Among them are, for example, mothers, who have long regarded hot dogs as instant worms to be poked down the clamoring craws of their fledglings. Also there are bachelorettes, who have traditionally held hot dogs in scorn, apparently considering them things to be eaten only at baseball games, and thus, never. The most sympathetic distaff group is that of the desperate brides. Like bachelors, they need all the help they can get.

All these categories of cooks—and any others, as well—are invited to check the recipes that follow. In light of the original audience, I have included a good deal of very basic material. Furthermore, the recipes will for the most part adhere to three important criteria. First, they will be quick—mostly under half an hour—involving as little work in the kitchen as possible. Secondly, they will rely primarily on mundane ingredients. No one is expected to have a ready stock of dried pears or fresh sturgeon eggs. Just onions, potatoes, cheese, and frankfurters. Finally, the recipes strive for flexibility. The more variations on and substitutions in any single dish the better. Whenever applicable, variations will be suggested.

The moment of this book's conception may explain most clearly its real purpose. While living out in the country in Brown County, Indiana, a poverty-ridden graduate student at Indiana University, I asked an afternoon date if she wanted to stay for supper.

She asked, "What are you having?"

"Hot dogs," I said tentatively.

Her response was immediate and direct: "Ecch!"

"All right, baby," I snarled at her, "sit down and I'll put hot dogs to you like you've never seen before."

That, innocuously enough, was the birth of Bowser Buns, a love affair, and the idea for this book.

Acknowledgments

I confess myself indebted to many, among whom the following loom large: David Andrew, Mary Boudreau, Ann Brown, Maya and Roy Chatterjee, Jane Chesebro, Devon Coles, Ann Crooker, Polly Fulle, Martha and Sally Holden, Madeline Jeppeson, Jordan's Ready-to-eat Meats, Inc., Buck Lade, Anne LeBlanc, Dean Paterson, Jane Petro, Margaret Ricci, Myrtle Russell, Clare Ruthenburg, Mrs. James Searles, Robert Shute, Sally Theberge, Mary Totman, and, of course, my family, who had to bear most of the brunt of the experimentation and judgment.

Harpswell, Maine
1972

Contents

Preface	vii
A Note on Hot Dogs	1
Hints and Prefatory Recipes	3
Hors d'Oeuvres	7
Breakfasts	17
Lunches	25
Dinners	59
Specialty Dishes	81
Glossary of Terms	93
Appendix A: Grocery List	95
Appendix B: Utensil List	99
Index	101

A NOTE ON HOT DOGS

Hot dogs are precooked, smoked sausages made from either pork and beef in combination or beef alone. There are several other variables in hot dog manufacture to consider when selecting brands.

The phrase "all meat" means that the hot dog is made from selected cuts of shoulder, flank, loin, and other skeletal meats. If a package is not marked "all meat," the choice meats have been diluted with "extenders"—milk powder, cereal, soy flour— or with "variety" meats—heart, liver, tongue. Into this last category falls the celebrated "chicken dog."

A second distinction is the hot dog's casing. After the meat has been ground and seasoned, it is stuffed into a tube and then cooked. Sometimes this tube (or casing) is made of washed and salted intestine—"natural casing." Otherwise, it is plastic. After the hot dog has been cooked, the plastic casing is removed to make a "skinless" hot dog.

Finally hot dogs differ as to their spices. Seasonings may include coriander, garlic, ground mustard, nutmeg, salt, sugar, and white pepper; which ones and in what proportions are matters of individual manufacturers. True connoisseurs will sample brands widely before casting their decisions.

In selecting brands, the cook ought to remember one fact. Just as there are cooking wines, so too are there many cooking uses for inferior hot dogs. Many of the recipes in this book do not require highest grade hot dogs. A good rule of thumb is the more ingredients (especially spicy ones), the lower quality of hot dog permissible.

The cook will often change hot dogs' forms when using this book. They can be cut into chunks or coins, into halves lengthwise or strips. They can be diced or minced with a knife. They can be ground with a meat grinder or chopped with a blender. They can be grated or shredded with a grater. This last process isn't difficult; simply grate the hot dog at one end, pushing it against the grater and keeping your fingers out of the way.

Because they are precooked, hot dogs may be eaten cold. They will keep for three weeks in the refrigerator, and for months in the freezer.

HINTS AND PREFATORY RECIPES

To experienced hands in the kitchen, most of this section will be old hat. To novices, however, this is the walk-before-you-run part of the curriculum.

The single most important piece of advice to a neophyte chef is "Get it all together—first." Don't cut or cook a thing until you have (1) all the ingredients lined up, (2) all the utensils laid out, (3) the recipe fresh in your mind, and (4) the oven (if you are baking) set on the temperature called for. The last item in this checklist is called "preheating." Unless you have one of those strange ovens that don't require it, remember it.

Another general bit of advice that informs this whole book is "Don't be fooled into taking recipes as Sacred Writ." If you're out of something, try something else. If you don't like a particular ingredient, substitute one that you do. And as far as measurements are concerned, be careful but be sensible as well. In most cases, a quarter teaspoon of flour one way or the other probably won't matter. I cooked for two years using a coffee cup and my eyeball to measure with.

Butter: I've used the word "butter" throughout this book, although margarine works just as well for my palate. Incidentally, there are markings on the wrappers of most margarine sticks, dividing each into tablespoons.

Eggs: Many of the recipes call for eggs cooked in special ways. "Poached" eggs are broken into a frying pan filled with salted, steaming water. A little vinegar in the water is supposed to keep the egg white from separating. "Boiled" eggs are immersed, while still in the shell, into boiling water. About five minutes after the water returns to a boil, they are soft-boiled; in ten more, they are hard-boiled. You can tell a raw egg from a hard-boiled one by spinning them. The latter turns faster and more easily.

Onions: A small onion when diced equals a half cup. A medium one is about twice that.

Potatoes: Potatoes, like eggs, can be boiled and stored in the refrigerator. Many of the recipes in this book assume the presence of boiled potatoes. Simply drop them, unpeeled, into boiling water. In about 30 to 40 minutes (depending on their size) a fork slips into them easily, and they are done. They will keep in their jackets for up to three weeks.

Fresh vegetables: These are generally cheaper than canned or frozen ones, but more work. They are cooked by boiling. Wash them in cool water and drop them into slightly salted boiling water. Cooking time varies with the particular vegetable, its size, and its age. Here are some typical ranges:

> Beets: 20–30 minutes
> Carrots: 15–20 minutes
> Corn: 10–20 minutes
> Peas: 10–15 minutes
> Green beans: 15–35 minutes

HORS D'OEUVRES

Hors d'oeuvre is a French phrase meaning, literally, "outside of the work." The "work," here, is dinner; outside of it are those introductory goodies normally washed down with before-dinner cocktails. Hors d'oeuvres can be plain or fancy, depending on the situation. The following recipes do not pretend to definitiveness in the hot dog hors d'oeuvres line. Hopefully, however, they will provide inspiration and assistance to the budding cocktail-party thrower.

HOT DOG PATE

An easy spread for Ritz crackers, melba toast, Triscuits, and so on.

> 2 hot dogs
> 3 ounces cream cheese

Grate the hot dogs. With a fork, work the meat and the cream cheese together well. Put into a shallow dish.

Variations: You can use cream cheese and olive mix, or cream cheese and chives. An interesting hors d'oeuvre is made from small squares of bread covered with this and broiled for just a moment. Sprinkle with paprika.

This mixture also makes good sandwiches. Especially with lettuce and mayonnaise.

PIGLETS IN BLANKETS

This is an hors d'oeuvre that looks much harder than it really is.

> ½ tube refrigerated crescent rolls
> 4 hot dogs
> 2–3 slices cheese

Unroll the crescent rolls and separate them into triangles. Put a hot dog on the wide end of each triangle and roll it up. Carefully cut the dough and the dog into ¼" to ½" chunks. Place the pieces on a cookie sheet with the meat running vertically. Cover with a small section of a cheese slice. Bake for about 10 minutes at 375° until the roll is brown. (Makes about 50.)

Variations: You can put other little goodies on top of the cheese: bits of olive, green pepper, pimento, etc.

For a tasty lunch, stuff the hot dog with cheese, then roll it up. Bake it cheese side up and serve hot.

DOGGIE THINS

Despite their name, these are reasonably fancy hors d'oeuvres. If you serve them at a black-tie affair, then, it might be better not to mention what they're called.

>1–2 hot dogs
>4–6 large stuffed olives
>3 slices American cheese
>3 slices thin-sliced bread

Slice the hot dog into coins, and the olives into stuffed rings. Lay a cheese slice over each piece of bread and trim off the crusts, so that the cheese completely covers the bread. Next, arrange the hot dog coins regularly in rows on the cheese, and put an olive slice on top of each.

With a large knife, carefully cut the slices of bread and cheese into small squares, leaving a piece of hot dog on each. Place the squares on a cookie sheet, and broil them for about 5 minutes. Cool and serve with toothpicks.

Variations: You can vary the cheese or the olives (by using black ones). Also try other ingredients—radishes, celery, etc.

DOG-DEVILED EGGS

A simple and appreciated offering to any hors d'oeuvres tray.

> 1 hot dog
> 6 eggs (boiled)
> 3 tablespoons mayonnaise
> Salt and pepper
> Paprika

Grate the hot dog. Remove the eggshells and slice the eggs in half along their long axes. Put the yolks and the hot dog into a mixing bowl. Add the mayonnaise, the salt and pepper; with a fork mash these together. Then restuff the whites and sprinkle the tops with paprika.

Variations: This recipe forms the core of an excellent sandwich. Merely mash the whites and the yolks together, along with everything else, and place it between 2 slices of bread, for a dog-egg-salad sandwich.

BATTERED BITS

Somewhat messy in preparation, these are more than worth the trouble in goodness and interest. The batter here can also be used to make fried clams.

4 hot dogs	2 eggs
¾ cup milk	1 cup bread crumbs or
1 cup flour	crushed crackers

Cut the hot dogs into inch chunks. In a bowl, mix the milk, the flour, and the eggs together until smooth. In a second dish, place the bread crumbs.

Dip the hot dog chunks into the batter, then roll them in the bread crumbs. Drop them into hot fat or cooking oil and fry them until brown. Serve warm, either from the oven or in a chafing dish, with toothpicks.

Variations: Made whole and served with ketchup or tartar sauce, these make a tasty lunch item.

DOGGIE BALLS

An excellent, all-around hors d'oeuvre.

- 4 hot dogs
- 2 egg whites
- 1 teaspoon cornstarch
- 1 tablespoon bread crumbs
- Soy sauce

Grate the hot dogs and mix them with the egg whites, the cornstarch, and the bread crumbs. Roll the mixture into balls and fry them in hot cooking oil. Pour soy sauce over them and serve. (Makes about 20 balls.)

Variations: Diced onions are delightful when mixed in with the dogs. This can make a neat sandwich, formed into a patty and fried. Also, other sauces are good here—Worcestershire, horseradish, ketchup, etc.

CREAM CHEESE POPS

A high caloric hors d'oeuvre. Remember, you can buy the cream cheese with olives already mixed in.

> 4 hot dogs
> 10 or so large stuffed olives
> 3-ounce package cream cheese
> Paprika

Gash the hot dogs lengthwise. Chop up the olives and with a fork blend them into the cream cheese. Then stuff the hot dogs and sprinkle paprika over them. Finally, cut the stuffed dogs into pieces roughly an inch long, and pierce each piece with a toothpick.

Variations: The olives may be omitted or replaced with chives, pimentos, or even candied fruit—orange rinds, maraschino cherries, or pineapple chunks.

SWISS CHEESE ROLL-UPS

Not only does this make luscious hors d'oeuvres, it can put luncheon guests into a tizzy as well. See the variations.

> 4 hot dogs
> 3 tablespoons mayonnaise
> 1 tablespoon sour cream
> ¼ teaspoon horseradish
> 5–6 slices Swiss cheese

Grate the hot dogs, and blend them with the mayonnaise, the sour cream, and the horseradish. Put a spoonful of the mixture on each of the slices of cheese and roll it up. Secure each with 4 toothpicks evenly spaced from one end of the roll to the other. The mixture may ooze out the holes, but don't worry. Cut the rolls into 4 sections between each toothpick.

Variations: American cheese, which breaks rather than rolls, doesn't work as well as Swiss. You are invited to experiment with other types. Also, try chopped onion or green pepper in the filling.

A neat lunch item (as promised above) is to place the rolled cheese, toothpicked once or twice, into a hot dog bun. Broil for 5–10 minutes, remove the picks, and serve.

POTTED DOGS

This hors d'oeuvre provides a good way of using up leftover wine—assuming, of course, that you ever have any leftover wine.

> 4 hot dogs
> 2 tablespoons butter
> 1 cup red burgundy wine

Cut the hot dogs into 1-inch chunks, while melting the butter in a frying pan. Place the hot dogs and the wine in the pan, cover, and simmer for 10–15 minutes. Serve them in the sauce, with cocktail picks, still warm. If possible, use a chafing dish.

Variations: You can use different wines here. A white wine, being lighter, will flavor the dogs more delicately. Chianti, on the other hand, leaves no doubt.

CURRANT DOGS

A quick, yummy toothpick treat.

> 6–8 hot dogs
> 10 ounces currant jelly (more or less)
> 1 tablespoon yellow mustard

Cut the hot dogs into 1-inch chunks. Heat the jelly and the mustard over low heat until the jelly melts. Add the hot dogs to the liquid and simmer for 10 minutes. If possible, serve in a chafing dish.

Variations: Feel free to experiment with the type of jelly. Also, here is a place to use those little cocktail franks. So is the following recipe.

SAUCED DOGS

The sauce here handles a large number of wee cocktail weenies. Thus, this recipe is best suited for parties on the order of receptions of state or class reunions.

> 2 pounds cocktail franks
> 1 small onion, diced
> 1 tablespoon butter
> ½ cup water
> 2 tablespoons cider vinegar
> 1 tablespoon Worcestershire sauce
> 2 tablespoons brown sugar
> 1 cup ketchup
> ½ teaspoon salt
> ¼ teaspoon pepper

Sauté the franks and the onions in the butter. And the remaining ingredients and heat for 15 minutes. Serve with toothpicks, hot, in a chafing dish if possible.

Variation: If you don't have any cocktail franks, use 1-inch chunks of standard dogs.

HOT DOG FONDUE

Fondue, derived from a French word meaning "melted," is an excellent, although rather complex, hors d'oeuvre. It requires a certain amount of paraphernalia, anyway, although you can, I suppose, substitute a Sterno stove and a saucepan for the alcohol burner and the fondue pot.

In any case, the easiest type of fondue is called "fondue bourguignonne." In the fondue pot (or whatever chafing dish you have set up), heat a cooking oil. Olive, peanut, and vegetable oils are most common; butter and margarine are possible. Using a long, thin fork, spear a chunk of hot dog (in this cookbook, anyhow —the others will say choice beef) and place it in the hot oil. When it is thoroughly heated, dunk it in one of the sauces described below and eat it.

SOUR CREAM AND HORSERADISH SAUCE

2 tablespoons sour cream
¼ teaspoon horseradish

Be *very* careful mixing in the horseradish. A little goes a long way.

RED SOUR CREAM AND ONION

1 tablespoon sour cream
1 tablespoon ketchup or cocktail sauce
½ teaspoon dried onion flakes

or

1 tablespoon onion dip

There are many other easy sauces. Do not overlook, for instance, the normal hot dog condiments—mustard, relish, and ketchup. Look around the supermarket. You'll be surprised at how many prepared sauces you'll find.

BREAKFASTS

Breakfast, essentially, is the first meal of the day. Existentially, it's much harder to define; breakfast to some people looks like dinner to others. I have stayed on the traditional side of the fence, figuring that the people who eat potatoes, beans, meat, and gravy in the morning don't need my help. I have tried only to show how hot dogs can be incorporated into the bacon-and-egg scene.

FRENCH TOASTED DOGS

Although the hot dogs on French toast may look like an afterthought, they don't taste like one.

4 hot dogs	3 tablespoons sugar
Butter	½ teaspoon salt
2 eggs	6 slices bread
1 cup milk	

Slice the hot dogs lengthwise into strips and brown them in butter in a frying pan. With a fork, mix well the eggs, the milk, the sugar, and the salt. Dip the bread in the batter and fry on both sides in a half inch of cooking oil. When the toast is done, cover it with the hot dog strips, and serve it with maple syrup. (Serves 2.)

Variation: The deep fat makes the toast crisp. For the softer, more traditional effect, cook it like regular pancakes.

HOT DOG PANCAKES

When working from scratch, I usually make cornmeal pancakes. But, because of the number of prepared pancake mixes around, the recipe below is for the more ambitious. Everybody else can grab an Aunt Jemima.

¾ cup boiling water
½ cup yellow cornmeal
1 tablespoon sugar
1 teaspoon salt
1 cup milk

1 cup all-purpose flour
2 teaspoons baking powder
2 hot dogs
2 eggs

Pour the boiling water over the cornmeal, the sugar, and the salt, and let stand for a couple of minutes, until the cornmeal swells. Then stir in the milk, the flour, and the baking powder. Grate the hot dogs into the mixture; and finally, stirring quickly, add the eggs.

Cook the pancakes on a hot, greased skillet. Serve with powdered sugar and maple syrup, honey, or jelly. (Serves 2.)

Variation: Deep-fat fried pancakes are puffy. Very good.

OMELETTE AU CHIEN CHAUD

A continental dish that has never been featured at Antoine's. Good, nonetheless.

1 hot dog
½ small onion
2 eggs
¼ cup grated Cheddar
 cheese

2 tablespoons butter
Salt and pepper

Grate the hot dog and dice the onion. Beat the eggs well, and stir in the hot dog, onion, and cheese. Melt the butter in a frying pan. Pour in the mixture, add salt and pepper, cover, and cook over a low fire. When a crust has formed on the bottom, use a knife to slash through. This allows the inside to cook more easily. (Serves 1.)

Variations: The omelet can be made more exciting by covering, while still in the frying pan, the top with jelly or marmalade and serving it folded over. You can top it with whipped cream if you desire.

SCRAMBLED DOGS

The biggest difference between scrambles and omelets is that the former are chopped up during cooking and the latter are not. Since the wetness of scrambled eggs is for many a subject more personal than religion or politics, I will say only that the more they are cooked, the drier they get.

- 2 hot dogs
- ½ small onion
- 1 tablespoon butter
- 4 eggs
- ½ cup light cream
- Salt and pepper
- Paprika

Grate the hot dogs and dice the onion. Sauté them in the butter until the onion starts to brown. Then mix the eggs and the cream with a fork, and pour them into the frying pan. When cooked, add the seasoning. (Serves 2.)

Variations: Green peppers, olives, and cheese can all be added to scrambled dogs.

POACHED EGGS ON HOT DOG HASH

Here is a tasty morning meal for those who possess *some* motor skills at that hour. Be careful not to grate your fingers.

½ small onion	1 medium potato (boiled)
2 tablespoons butter	Salt and pepper
4 hot dogs	4 eggs

Dice the onion and sauté it in the butter for 5 minutes. Meanwhile, grate the hot dogs, and chop the potato into small chunks. Add them, along with salt and pepper, to the sautéed onion; mix the whole; and brown it.

Poach the eggs. Make piles of the hot dog hash on plates and place an egg on each. (Serves 2.)

Variations: The main variations will change the title. Fried or boiled eggs will work fine; and the hash can be served beside scrambled eggs, also.

SOFT-BOILED EGGS WITH CREAMED DOGS

A delicious breakfast dish. If you really want to celebrate something in the morning, serve this with some Rhine wine.

2 hot dogs	¼ teaspoon salt
1 small onion	4 eggs
1 tablespoon butter	4 slices toast or 2 English muffins
1 tablespoon flour	
1 cup milk or light cream	

Cut the hot dogs into small pieces and dice the onion. Melt the butter in a frying pan, and sauté the onion until it starts to brown. Add the flour, the milk or cream, and the salt. Stir until the mixture is creamy; then add the hot dog chunks. Simmer for 5 minutes.

Meanwhile, soft-boil the eggs, and serve them on the toast or muffins. Cover them with the creamed hot dogs. (Serves 2.)

Variations: You can use creamed dogs on fried, poached, or baked eggs.

HOT DOGS AND SHIRRED EGGS

"Shirred," when applied to eggs, means "baked." To be totally proper, shirred eggs are supposed to be served in individual baking dishes. Nuts. A casserole works fine.

3 hot dogs	4 eggs
2 tablespoons butter	Salt and pepper
3 tablespoons relish	Paprika

Dice the hot dogs finely, and sauté them in butter 5–10 minutes. Remove from fire. Mix in the relish. Place this mixture in the baking dish(es).

Carefully break the eggs into the dish(es). Add the seasonings. Bake for about 15 minutes at 350°. (Serves 2.)

Variations: Many, many possibilities exist to replace or augment the relish: ketchup, apple slices and brown sugar, potatoes and/or onions, bacon, bread crumbs.

EGGS BENEDOGGED

Based on eggs Benedict, this dish is of a lower order—and much easier.

> 4 hot dogs
> Butter
> 4 slices toast
> 4 eggs
> 4 slices American cheese

Slice the hot dogs lengthwise in strips and brown them in butter in a frying pan. Lay them on the toast. Fry the eggs (sunny side up is best, unless you require a solidly cooked yolk) and lay them on the hot dog strips. Cover the eggs with cheese and broil until the cheese starts to brown. (Serves 2.)

Variations: Aside from substituting types of cheeses, poached eggs may be exchanged for fried; English muffins for toast; and hollandaise sauce for cheese. There are good instant hollandaise mixes on the market. (If you substitute all of these, plus ham for the hot dogs, you will have, of course, eggs Benedict.)

HOT DOG CRÊPES

Crêpes, light thin pancakes served rolled around a filling, make fancy breakfasts or lunches. My favorite French chef, Anne LeBlanc, graciously supplied the following crêpe recipe.

2 tablespoons butter	½ cup flour
1 cup milk	½ teaspoon salt
2 eggs	1 teaspoon baking powder

Heat the butter and the milk together in a saucepan. When they are mixed, allow them to cool. Beat the eggs and add them to the saucepan, mixing in the flour, the salt, and the baking powder. The resulting batter should be thin and smooth.

When cooking a crêpe, pour a couple of tablespoons of batter into a greased, medium-hot frying pan and tilt it, coating the bottom. Turn once. Keep the crêpes in a warm oven until all are done and the filling is ready.

FILLING

2 hot dogs
2 tablespoons butter
1–2 tablespoons flour
1 cup milk or light cream
Paprika
Salt and pepper

Dice the hot dogs finely. Melt the butter in a saucepan, blend in the flour, and stir in the milk or cream slowly. When the mixture is creamy and thick, add the seasonings and the hot dogs. (Serves 2.)

Variations: For dessert, fill the crêpes with, say, raspberry jam, and sprinkle them with powdered sugar. The hot dog filling above can be varied by adding vegetables—peas, diced carrots, onions.

LUNCHES

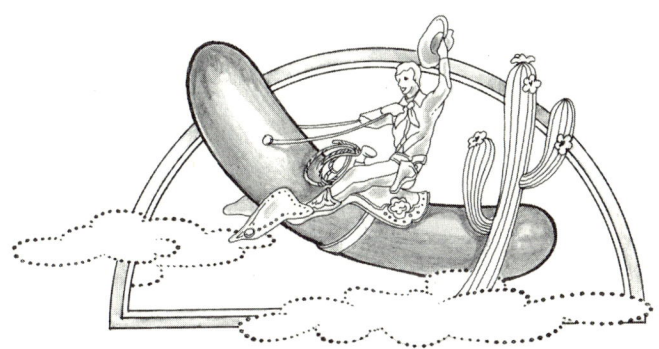

A lunch, to my mind, is a light meal. Although you can serve any of the following recipes at any time of day, each of them can fit happily somewhere into my idea of a luncheon menu. A particular recipe may suffice for the whole meal or not, depending on the recipe itself and the appetites of the lunchers. You'll have to learn to judge these factors and supplement the skimpy ones with salads, soups, rolls, desserts, and so on.

HOT DOG SANDWICHES

Since John Montagu, the fourth Earl of Sandwich, began putting meat between bread, sandwiches are almost synonymous with lunches. So, this title seems like a good place to start this section. The traditional avatar of a hot dog—i.e., grilled and stuffed in a bun like a well-browned baby in its blanket—is itself, loosely speaking, a sandwich. But we can go beyond this.

Cold, the hot dog tastes somewhat like Bologna, and, indeed, the two sausages are very similar. Thus, hot dogs can be sliced lengthwise into strips and used as sandwich meat along with cheese, lettuce, and mayonnaise or mustard. Frying the strips adds a delicate touch of goodness.

In the hors d'oeuvres section, I suggested the dog-egg-salad sandwiches; and with the idea of grating hot dogs emerges a host of other possibilities. For instance, mix grated hot dog and sandwich spread together and place between slices of toast—with lettuce and tomato if you wish. Another great sandwich requires grated hot dog, sliced olives (green and black), diced onion, pieces of tomato, cheese, and green pepper. Place all these ingredients in a bun and pour olive oil, salt, and pepper over them.

A few other sandwich recipes follow. Hot dog sandwich—that's earl, Brother.

HOT HOT DOG SANDWICHES

The Poor Man's Best Friend becomes better in this recipe.

- 4 hot dogs
- ½ green pepper
- 1 small onion
- ¼ cup chopped celery or cucumber
- ¼ cup mayonnaise
- 1 teaspoon lemon juice or vinegar
- ½ teaspoon Worcestershire sauce
- 8 slices bread

Grate the hot dogs, and dice the pepper and the onion. Place these ingredients, plus the celery or cucumber, in a frying pan and sauté for 5 minutes. Remove from heat; add the mayonnaise, the lemon juice or vinegar, and the Worcestershire; and blend the whole well. Spread the mixture on the bread and make sandwiches. Broil on each side for 3–5 minutes. (Serves 2.)

Variations: Grated cheese over the top is not necessary but very good. Toasted bread can be used instead of broiled, or the sandwiches can be wrapped in aluminum foil and baked (400° for 8–10 minutes). Also you can use buns in place of the bread.

PEANUT PUP SANDWICH

I admit this sounds a bit strange, but don't eschew it until you've chewed it.

4 hot dogs	8 slices bread
Butter	Peanut butter
4 slices cheese	

Cut the hot dogs into thin strips lengthwise, and fry them in butter until they are well browned—almost crisp. Then use them to make sandwiches with the cheese, the peanut butter, and the bread. Grill the sandwiches before serving. (Makes 4 sandwiches.)

Variations: All the cooking variations in the previous recipe work here as well. The sandwiches can be modified with the addition of lettuce and mayonnaise. Try it.

HOT DOG SALAD SANDWICH

If you don't have a blender, use a meat grinder or grate the hard ingredients and chop them finely.

2 hot dogs	½ cup mayonnaise
½ small onion, diced	Salt and pepper
½ cup chopped celery	Paprika
¼ cup grated Cheddar cheese	8 slices bread

Cut the hot dogs into small chunks, and put all the ingredients except the bread into a blender. Run the blender at a medium-slow speed until everything is mixed into a spread. This is the essence of a super sandwich. (Makes 4 sandwiches.)

Variations: This is also a good chip dip. It can receive extra sparkle from a shot of horseradish, mustard, or other condiment.

BAGEL DOGS

This recipe *should* be served with all-beef hot dogs.

>   4 hot dogs   Horseradish sauce
>   2 bagels   2 slices cheese

Slice the hot dogs lengthwise in half. Split the bagels and spread them with the horseradish. Cut the hot dog halves into short pieces, fit them onto the bagel halves, and cover with cheese. Broil for 5–8 minutes until brown. (Serves 2.)

Variations: Vary the condiments (mustard, ketchup, etc.) and add other ingredients (tomato, lettuce, onion, etc.).

CRUNCHY HOT DOGS

An exciting and dumfoundingly simple maneuver, somewhat similar to Battered Bits (q.v.).

>   2 tablespoons ketchup   1 cup finely crushed Ritz
>   1 tablespoon mustard   crackers
>   4 hot dogs

Mixing the ketchup and the mustard, roll the hot dogs first in the mixture, and then in the crushed crackers. Bake for 15 minutes at 400°. Next broil for another minute or so. Serve in hot dog rolls, in slices of bread, or plain. (Serves 2.)

Variations: Use other condiments—relish, barbecue sauce, etc. Bread crumbs or crushed potato chips work well in place of the crackers.

DOWN-EAST HOT DOG CHOWDER

This believe-it-or-not item was suggested by a friend in a fit of hysterical laughter. Thus challenged, I whipped it up, modeling it on clam chowder, and found it extremely good, although mild.

> 4 hot dogs
> 1 medium onion
> 4 tablespoons butter
> 1 medium potato
> 1 tablespoon flour
> 1 cup water
> 3 cups milk
> Salt and pepper
> Paprika

Cut the hot dogs into 1-inch pieces, and dice the onion finely. Sauté them in the butter for 5 minutes. Meanwhile, cut the potato into pieces slightly smaller than the hot dogs. Add the potato, the flour, and the water to the hot dogs and onions. Cover and cook over a slow fire until the potato is done (15–20 minutes).

Heat the milk to near the boiling point. Put the chowder into a serving bowl and pour the milk over it. Season to taste. (Serves 4.)

Variations: Many canned or cooked fresh vegetables (corn, beans, peas, carrots, etc.) can be added to the chowder after the potato is done.

Chowder tastes even better after a day or so of aging.

EGG-DOG SOUP

Many soups can be enhanced by adding cut-up hot dogs. Below is just such a treat, weird-looking but great-tasting; and below that is a list of other suggestions.

>   2 hot dogs
>   1 can beef bouillon
>   2 eggs

Cut up the hot dogs into small pieces and put them into the bouillon. Bring the soup to a full boil. While the soup is still on the fire, break the egg into it. It will scatter immediately into little bits of cooked egg. (Serves 2.)

Variations: In making soup for 2 people, remember that you do not have to add a full can of water to condensed soups. A half can will usually give the right proportions and still cut the soup enough.

Hot dogs go well with pea, tomato, vegetable, and cream of mushroom soups. Experiment a bit. You'll find more.

BOWSER BUNS

These can be ripped off in no time and with less effort. If you already have some potatoes boiled up, try this recipe. If not, head for the next page.

>   3 hot dogs
>   Butter
>   1 medium potato (boiled)
>   Cheese

Grate the hot dogs and the potato into a mixing bowl and mix. Form them into patties and fry in butter on a medium fire. As soon as you turn the patties, cover them with cheese. (Makes 4 buns.)

Variations: Diced onions, green peppers, etc., are good mixed in. Instead of cheese, you can use sour cream, sauces, or gravies to top the buns off. If you're a ketchup freak, consider using that, for instance.

PUPPY PIES

A bit more sophisticated than Bowser Buns, these emerge looking somewhat like swallows' nests. Serve them to your arty friends.

2 medium potatoes	1 tablespoon flour
3 hot dogs	½ teaspoon salt
1 egg	

Peel the potatoes, and grate them and the hot dogs together into a mixing bowl. Add the egg, the flour, and the salt, and mix well.

In a frying pan, heat ¼" cooking oil or fat until it is very hot. Drop tablespoons of the mixture into the fat and cook until the pies are golden brown on both sides. (Serves 4.)

Variations: You can add onion or green pepper; you can serve with gravy; or you can make one big puppy pie using all the mixture at once and cover it with vegetables, for a truly unique vegetable pie.

PUFFY PUPPIES

Serve these with a salad; they're delightful.

>   4 hot dogs
>   1 small onion
>   2 eggs
>   3 ounces cream cheese
>   ½ cup mayonnaise

Slice the hot dogs in half lengthwise, and lay them in a casserole. Slice the onion and put it over the hot dog halves. Separate the eggs. This is done by breaking each egg carefully in half and pouring, even more carefully, the yolk back and forth between the halves of the eggshell, allowing the white to drop into a bowl underneath.

Mix the yolks, the cream cheese, and the mayonnaise together. Beat the whites well, and fold them into the cream cheese mixture. Pour over ingredients in the casserole. Bake for 15–20 minutes at 375°. (Serves 2.)

Variations: You can flavor this dish with horseradish, garlic, or chives. Or try substituting relish for the onions.

COLEDOG SLAW

A new version of an old chestnut, this slaw can be served with sandwiches for lunch or with baked beans and brown bread for supper. If the latter, cut back to one hot dog in the slaw and put others in the beans.

2 hot dogs
¼ head cabbage
¼ cup vinegar
3 tablespoons mayonnaise
Salt and pepper
Paprika

Chop the hot dogs and the cabbage together. Mix the vinegar and the mayonnaise until creamy, and then stir them into the cabbage and hot dogs. Add the seasonings. (Serves 2.)

Variations: Slaw can be made more interesting by the addition of raisins, chopped nuts, shredded carrots, or small quantities of chopped canned or fresh fruits. Incidentally, the mayonnaise can be cut with water if no vinegar is available.

H.D. POTATO SALAD

Potato salad, a perennial crowd-pleaser, has the added advantage of lasting long in the refrigerator. Make it this week and serve it the next.

3 hot dogs
3 medium potatoes (boiled)
1 medium onion
6–8 stuffed olives
4 eggs (hard-boiled)
3 tablespoons mayonnaise
Salt and pepper
Paprika
Chives
Lettuce

Cut the hot dogs into small pieces and the potatoes into slightly larger chunks. Dice the onion and the olives. Chop the eggs into these ingredients with a spoon, and then mix in the mayonnaise, adding it a tablespoonful at a time. Finally, put in the seasonings, and serve salad on leaves of lettuce. (Serves 4.)

Variations: The range of potato salad can be extended by adding such ingredients as cheese, tomatoes, celery, or leftover vegetables like green beans, peas, or carrots.

HOT DOG MACARONI SALAD

An easy-to-make quickie that can be thrown together several days ahead of time.

- 2–3 hot dogs
- 2 cups cooked macaroni
- 3 tablespoons mayonnaise
- 1 tablespoon water
- Salt and pepper
- Paprika
- Lettuce

Cut the hot dogs into small chunks and mix with the macaroni in a salad bowl. In a small cup, mix the mayonnaise and the water, and pour the resulting sauce over the salad. Toss the salad and season well. Chill it. Serve on a leaf of lettuce. (Serves 2.)

Variations: You can use any noodle product for this salad. If you use spaghetti or vermicelli, however, break it into smaller pieces before you cook it. Cooked or canned vegetables, especially peas, are very good mixed in.

TOSSED SALAD

Although this can go very well with larger meals, by itself it can make a classy light lunch or supper. A white wine—a Rhine or a Chablis, e.g.—will have guests eating out of your hand (figuratively speaking, at least). Great for hot days.

3 hot dogs	1 stalk celery
2 tomatoes	½ small cucumber
1 small onion (white or red)	2 eggs (hard-boiled)
2· radishes	Lettuce
½ green pepper	Salad dressing
Slice of cheese	Salt and pepper
6–8 stuffed olives	Paprika

Cut up separately the hot dogs, the tomatoes, the onion, the radishes, the green pepper, the cheese, the olives, the celery, the cucumber, and the eggs. Break the lettuce into bite-sized leaves.

If you are serving from a single bowl, put in everything except the cucumber and the eggs. Add the dressing and toss. Garnish the bowl with the cucumber and the eggs. Then add the seasonings.

If you are setting out individual servings, arrange the ingredients in bowls, beginning with the lettuce and continuing as your artistic fancy dictates. Put the dressing and seasonings on last. (The ingredients above will make a single salad that will serve 4, or individual servings for 2.)

Variations: No dish admits to as many variations as a salad. Virtually anything will go in, and there are many different types of dressing on the market.

CAPE COD CRANBERRY DOG SALAD

From the bogs to the dogs!

4 hot dogs	Salt and pepper
1 cup cubed cranberry jelly	½ cup mayonnaise
1 cup diced celery	Lettuce
1 tablespoon lemon juice	

Dice the hot dogs. Place them in a mixing bowl with the jelly, the celery, the lemon juice, and the salt and pepper. Chill thoroughly. Then mix in the mayonnaise. Arrange the salad on lettuce leaves. (Serves 4.)

Variation: This can also be made with cranberry sauce, with the extra delight of whole cranberries.

BARBECUED DOGS

Here is a concession to those who may have been clamoring for a hot-dog-in-a-bun recipe.

1 small onion	1 cup barbecue sauce
¼ green pepper	½ cup water
4 hot dogs	4 buns
2 tablespoons butter	

Dice the onion and the green pepper; and, in a frying pan, sauté them along with the hot dogs in the butter. When the hot dogs start to brown, add the liquids, cover, and simmer for 15 minutes. Serve the hot dogs on the buns, covering them with the sauce.

Variations: These can also be served on top of rice or potatoes. Particularly good are sliced boiled potatoes simmered along with the dogs and sauce. Cut up the dogs if you wish.

CHILI DOGS

Supermarkets feature many brands of chili beans. If you buy one, check first the label, omitting any ingredients in this recipe that are redundant.

- ½ small onion
- ½ pound ground beef
- 2 tablespoons butter
- 4–6 hot dogs
- 8-ounce can tomatoes
- Small (approx. 10-ounce) can kidney beans
- ½ teaspoon salt
- 1 tablespoon (more or less) chili powder
- 4–6 hot dog buns

Dice the onion, and sauté it, together with the ground beef, in the butter. Add the hot dogs, the tomatoes, the beans, the salt, and the chili powder. Cover and simmer for 15–20 minutes. Sometime during the cooking process, taste the mixture to see if you have used enough chili powder.

To serve, partially fill each bun with the chili bean mixture. Then place a hot dog in the bun. (Serves 2–4.)

Variations: You can cut the hot dogs into chunks and serve the chili in a bowl with crackers over rice. Incidentally, green pepper is good in chili. Finally, if you don't have any ground beef, you can make a truly unique, desperation chili, using grated hot dogs in place of it.

PIZZA PUPPY TOASTS

Hot dogs and pizza fit together in many ways. A simple task is a hot dog pizza made from a mix or a frozen pizza crust. Here are some more ideas.

4 hot dogs	4 slices bread
1 tomato	2 tablespoons grated
¼ teaspoon garlic salt	Parmesan cheese
¼ teaspoon orégano	2 tablespoons grated
¼ teaspoon pepper	American cheese
Butter	

Grate the hot dogs. Chop the tomato finely, and blend it with the garlic salt, the orégano, and the pepper. Butter the bread slices and spread them with the tomato mixture. Then cover the tomato with the cheeses and the hot dogs. Bake at 400° for 10 minutes. (Serves 2.)

Variations: You can make a sauce by simmering the tomato, the cheeses, the butter, and the spices. Serve it either over hot dogs in a bun or over hot dogs and rice.

Cut into small squares, these make excellent hors d'oeuvres.

SLOPPY DOG ON A BUN

Remember those awful Sloppy Joes in your high-school cafeteria? Well, here's new taste to old waste—made possible by replacing hamburg with muttburg.

```
4 hot dogs                    1 16-ounce can tomatoes
1 medium onion                Salt and pepper
½ green pepper                4 hamburger buns
1 tablespoon butter
```

Grate the hot dogs and dice the onion and the green pepper. Sauté these ingredients in the butter for 5 minutes. Chop up the tomatoes, and add them, along with the salt and pepper, to the frying pan. Cover and simmer for another 5 minutes or so. Serve over the toasted buns. (Serves 2.)

Variations: Put cheese on the buns when you toast them, or sprinkle the Joes with grated cheese.

STUFFED TOMATOES

These are much like Stuffed Green Peppers in preparation, but they are a bit more delicate, requiring a lighter touch.

```
4 hot dogs                    Orégano
1 small onion                 4 tomatoes
½ green pepper                ½ cup grated cheese
2 tablespoons butter          ½ cup bread crumbs or
Salt and pepper                  crushed crackers
```

Grate the hot dogs and dice the onion and the green pepper. Sauté them in the butter and spices until the onion turns translucent and glossy. Carefully cut off the tops of the tomatoes, and scoop out the pulp. Turn them upside down on a paper towel to drain. Mix the cheese and the bread crumbs or crackers together. Fill the tomato shells ¾ of the way up with the hot dog mixture. Then fill them the rest of the way with the cheese and bread crumbs. Bake them in a bread pan or on a cookie sheet for 20–25 minutes at 375°. (Serves 4.)

Variations: Add some crumbled bacon to the hot dogs for crispness. Olives and/or pimentos are excellent in place of green peppers (but do not have to be sautéed).

STUFFED DOGS

A lady I know, discovering that I was writing this book, asked me to give her a recipe for a huge party she was throwing. I came up with this. The lady was grateful, but her cook, after preparing 300 stuffed dogs, was ready to sauté me. (Incidentally, for 150 guests, multiply the ingredients by 75.)

1 small onion
¼ green pepper
5 stuffed olives
4 hot dogs
½ cup grated Cheddar cheese
4 strips bacon

Dice fine the onion and the green pepper, and sauté for 5 minutes. Chop up and add the olives to the sautéed vegetables.

Gash the hot dogs lengthwise and fill them with the mixture. Then cover stuffing with the grated cheese.

Wrap each dog with a strip of bacon, securing the ends with a toothpick. Broil the dogs until the bacon is brown and crisp. (Serves 2.)

Variations: Many variations are possible, especially if you don't happen to have all the ingredients on hand. You can try messing around with bread crumbs. You can also try such condiments as relish, pickles, etc. One variation is important enough to be treated per se, below.

SPUD PUPS

Here is an easy variant on Stuffed Dogs. It can be made even easier if you have instant potatoes on hand. (In that case, figure about 1 ounce of potatoes per dog.)

1 medium potato	4 hot dogs
½ small onion	1 slice American cheese
¼ teaspoon salt	Paprika
1 tablespoon butter	Pepper
¼ cup milk	

Boil the potato. It is possible, in a pinch, to use cold boiled potatoes, but be warned that they will probably be lumpy when mashed. Remove the jacket and mash; a fork works fine as a masher. Dice the onion and blend it into the potato. Turn in the salt and butter. Then warm the milk and turn it in also until the potato is creamy.

Gash the hot dogs and stuff them with the potato mixture. Lay strips of cheese along the top, and put the spices over the cheese. Broil the dogs until the cheese melts and the top turns brown. (Serves 2.)

Variations: Different cheeses will make different versions. Try grated Parmesan, Cheddar, brick, or Swiss. Also, try this wrapped in bacon.

STUFFED POTATOES

Although baking the potatoes is a lengthy task, these have one advantage: they can be made well in advance. If such is the case, stuff them and put them in the refrigerator. Before serving, heat them for about 15 minutes, and then cover with cheese and broil. Serve with a salad.

2 medium potatoes	½ teaspoon salt
2 hot dogs	¼ teaspoon pepper
1 small onion	1 slice American cheese
4 stuffed olives	Paprika
¼ cup milk	

Poke a hole in each of the potatoes and bake them at 350° for an hour or so. Test them by sticking a fork in them; if it goes in easily, they are done. Lay the potatoes on a counter and remove the tops of the jackets by cutting an oval from the top side of each. Take out the potato meat carefully, without ripping the jackets.

Grate the hot dogs, and dice the onion and olives. Mix the potato meat, the hot dogs, the onion, the olives, the milk, the salt, and the pepper together so that the mixture is smooth. Stuff the jackets. Cover each potato with cheese and place each under a broiler until the cheese melts. Sprinkle the melted cheese with paprika. (Serves 2.)

Variations: These can be pepped up by substituting sour cream for milk and by adding other spices or condiments. Horseradish is good, for example.

SWEET POTATO BOATS

The sweet side of Stuffed Potatoes.

2 sweet potatoes (or yams)	2 tablespoons butter
2 hot dogs	½ teaspoon salt
2 slices bacon	¼ teaspoon pepper
½ cup chopped walnuts	

Poke a hole in each potato and bake them at 375° for about an hour, until a fork slides into them easily. Lay the potatoes on a counter and remove the tops of the jackets by cutting an oval from the top side of each. Take out the potato meat carefully, without ripping the jackets.

Dice the hot dogs and sauté them with the bacon until the

bacon is crisp. Drain the meats. Blend the potato meat, the hot dogs, the bacon (crumbled), the walnuts, the butter, and the seasonings. Stuff the jackets. Serve hot, reheating if necessary. (Serves 2.)

Variations: These may be sweetened to advantage by adding a tablespoon of brown sugar. Garnish them with sweet fruits—pineapple, maraschino cherries, candied fruits, etc.—and with bits of marshmallow. Cheese can add a nice touch.

DOG IN A FOXHOLE

A ridiculously easy maneuver but, once you get the idea, one that admits to all kinds of experimenting.

> 2 large potatoes
> 2 hot dogs
> Sour cream

With an apple corer or a paring knife, cut a "foxhole" into each potato. Stick the hot dogs into the foxholes and bake for 50–60 minutes at 350° until a fork enters the potatoes easily. Serve with sour cream. (Serves 2.)

Variations: You can make more than one hole and either cut the hot dog in half or use more than one. Make a potato-hot dog sculpture.

Try any of the variations on stuffed hot dogs. Be careful that the stuffing doesn't get all over the oven.

HOT DOG POTATO GRAVY

To make mashed potatoes, see Spud Pups. To make them better, serve with this gravy.

6 hot dogs	1 cup milk
3 slices bacon	Salt and pepper
3 tablespoons flour	4 servings mashed potatoes

Grate the hot dogs and dice the bacon. Sauté them until the bacon browns. Remove them from the fire and drain on paper towels. Save 2 tablespoons of the drippings.

Add the flour to the drippings and blend well. Then add the milk, stir, and bring to a boil. Finally, throw in the salt, the pepper, and the meat. Serve over the mashed potatoes. (Serves 4).

Variations: Other ingredients (diced onion, green pepper, etc.) are admissible. Furthermore, you can serve this with noodles, or even with toast. Broil some cheese on the toast first.

SHEEP DOG'S PIE

Remarkably simple, here is a hot dog version of Shepherd's Pie. It is a good way to use up leftover mashed potatoes.

4 hot dogs	1 tablespoon butter
1 cup beef broth, gravy, or bouillon	Paprika
2 cups (more or less) mashed potatoes (see Spud Pups)	

Cut the hot dogs into 1- to 2-inch chunks and place in a casserole dish. Add the liquid and spread mashed potatoes over the top. Dot with butter and paprika. Bake for 15–20 minutes at 375°. (Serves 2.)

Variations: Lots of additions are possible: onions, carrots, green beans, corn, name it.

HOT DOG WAGGLE

This is based on a shellfish recipe. If you try it with shrimp, it's a "wiggle."

4 hot dogs	1 cup light cream or milk
2 tablespoons butter	8-ounce can of peas
1–2 tablespoons flour (*depending on the thickness of the liquid*)	Salt and pepper
	Crisp crackers
	Paprika

Cut the hot dogs in half lengthwise and then into chunks. Melt the butter and blend in the flour. Stir in the cream or milk. Add and heat the peas and the hot dog chunks. Add salt and pepper to taste. Serve the waggle over the crackers, and sprinkle it with paprika. (Serves 2.)

Variations: Although peas are *de rigueur* for wiggles, there's no reason in a waggle why you can't use other vegetables: beans, carrots, asparagus, or mixed vegetables. It can be served on foods other than crackers: toast, rice, or noodles.

CREAMED CORN AND DOGS

The obvious way to make this is to use cream style corn. A less obvious, almost as easy, and tastier method appears below.

    2–3 hot dogs   1 cup cooked or canned
    ½ cup heavy cream   corn
    1 tablespoon flour   4 slices toast
    1 tablespoon butter   Pepper
    1 teaspoon sugar   Paprika
    ½ teaspoon salt

Cut the hot dogs into small chunks. In a saucepan, heat and mix the cream, the flour, the butter, the sugar, and the salt. Add the corn and the hot dogs, and bring the sauce to a slow boil, stirring constantly. Serve over the toast and season. (Serves 2.)

Variations: You can sauté the hot dog chunks first if you wish. Lighter creams may be substituted, but you'll need more flour. Peas or beans will do beautifully here as well.

CREAMED CHIPPED DOGS

Straight from camp—summer, boot, whatever—here is a new trick when applied to an old dog. Try it on toast.

    3–4 hot dogs   ½ teaspoon salt
    2 tablespoons butter   ¼ teaspoon pepper
    1 tablespoon flour   Paprika
    1½ cups light cream

Grate the hot dogs and sauté them in the butter until the chips begin to brown. Add the flour, and mix well. Add the cream, the salt, and the pepper. Stir and bring the mixture to a boil. Reduce heat, cover, and simmer for 5 minutes. When serving, sprinkle paprika over the top. (Serves 2.)

Variation: Add a bit of white wine for a kicker, *after* the mixture comes to a boil.

HOT DOG NEWBURG

If you are ever in the position to afford lobster, this is also a recipe for that kind of Newburg. Use 2 cups of cooked lobster meat.

4 hot dogs	½ teaspoon paprika
2 tablespoons butter	¼ cup sherry
1–2 eggs	Salt
½ cup heavy cream	4 slices toast

Dice the hot dogs and sauté them for 5 minutes in the butter. Separate the yolk (see Puffy Puppies) discarding the white. Beat together the yolk and the cream, and add them to the hot dogs. Cook this mixture over a medium fire, stirring until the cream thickens. Do not allow it to boil. (If it does, the Newburg will still be edible—it will just look grainy.) Add the paprika, the sherry, and the salt. Serve over buttered toast. (Serves 2.)

Variations: With 3 egg yolks, you can get away with milk instead of cream. You can serve this over rice, crackers, or noodles.

MACARONI, CHEESE, AND DOGS

An easy, reheatable casserole for a lunch or light supper, this dish can be served alone or with a salad.

1 cup macaroni	½ cup bread crumbs
4 hot dogs	¼ cup grated cheese
½ cup milk	Salt and pepper
4 slices cheese	Paprika
2 tablespoons butter	

Boil the macaroni according to the directions on the package. Since it will be cooked further, leave it slightly undercooked. Slice the hot dogs and heat them with the milk, the cheese slices, and the butter, until all the solids have melted. Drain the macaroni and add the cheese sauce, mixing well.

Turn the mixture into a casserole dish and sprinkle the top with the bread crumbs, the grated cheese, and the seasonings. Bake it at 400° for 10–15 minutes, until the top is browned. (Serves 2.)

Variations: You can, of course, use different cheeses (I prefer Cheddar). Also, cooked tomatoes or other vegetables can be thrown in for variety.

HOT DOG AND APPLE CUM CHEESE

This contains all the virtues of Eve's fruit: keeps doctors away, makes you a teacher's pet (if you happen to know one), and leads young ladies unto temptation. Good, too.

3–4 hot dogs	1 tablespoon butter
1 apple	Mustard
¾ tablespoons brown sugar	2 slices cheese

Slice the hot dogs in half lengthwise. Peel, core, and slice the apple. Lay the apple slices in a frying pan, putting the brown sugar and butter on top. Top the apple with hot dog, and spread each half thinly with mustard.

Cover the frying pan, and simmer for 10 minutes. Place the cheese slices over the dogs, re-cover, and simmer for 5 more minutes. (Serves 2.)

Variations: There are many other fruits possible in this recipe. Consider using peaches, apricots, or bananas.

SAVORY HOT DOG BREAD PUDDING

This came originally from England, via one of Mary Totman's English aunts. Upon arrival, it was ceremoniously hot-dogged.

4 hot dogs	½ cup milk
1 small onion	1–2 tablespoons butter
4 slices bread	½ cup grated Cheddar cheese
1 cup diced Cheddar cheese	
1 teaspoon seasoned salt	

Chop the hot dogs into coins, slice the onion thinly, and cut the bread into inch squares. Cover the bottom of a casserole dish with the squares from *two* slices of bread. Make layers of hot dogs, onion slices, diced cheese, and seasoned salt, covering finally with the remaining bread. Pour in the milk, which should come up to the onions. Dot the top with butter, and sprinkle with grated cheese. Bake for 25–30 minutes at 350°. You may turn on the broiler for the last couple of minutes to brown the top. (Serves 2.)

Variations: More substantial vegetables may be added, as well as bits of cooked bacon.

HOT DOG BISCUITS

These are good with any meal. If you have prepared biscuit mix, like Bisquick, use that; but if you're caught short, here is a reasonably simple recipe.

2 hot dogs
1 cup flour
½ teaspoon salt
1½ teaspoons baking powder
2 tablespoons butter
⅓ cup milk

Grate the hot dogs into a mixing bowl. Over them, sift together the flour, the salt, and the baking powder. Cut the butter into the dry ingredients with a pastry cutter or, lacking that, a fork. Add the milk slowly, stirring well, until the dough falls from the sides of the bowl.

Put the dough on a lightly floured board, and pat it until it is ½" to ¼" thick. Cut the biscuits with a small glass, a Dixie cup, or a frozen orange juice can. Place them on a greased cookie sheet, and bake them at 450° for about 10 minutes until brown. (Makes about 8 biscuits.)

Variation: You can make hush puppies that almost bark out loud by using hot dogs. Roll the biscuit dough into balls about 1½" in diameter and fry them in deep fat until brown.

CORN MUFFIN SURPRISES

If possible use corn bread mixes. They're good and easy. If impossible, use this recipe—it's good and not too tough.

3 hot dogs
2 eggs
2 tablespoons melted butter or fat
½ cup milk
⅔ cup flour
¾ cup cornmeal (either white or yellow)
2 teaspoons baking powder
2 tablespoons sugar
½ teaspoon salt

Cut each hot dog into 4 chunks. Grease a 12-muffin pan, and stand a piece of hot dog upright in each muffin mold. Beat together the eggs, the butter or fat, and the milk. Mix in the flour, the cornmeal, the baking powder, the sugar, and the salt. Pour the batter over each hot dog, filling about three-fourths of the mold. Bake at 400° for 25 minutes. (Makes 12 muffins.)

Variations: For less grainy corn bread, use ¾ cup flour and ⅔ cup cornmeal. A tablespoon of honey does delightful things to the batter.

Other ideas in this area: arrange whole hot dogs like wheel

spokes in a round, greased baking pan, and cover them with batter. Corn bread, furthermore, will work like a crust, so you can take something like Hot Dogs and Apples (*cum* or *sine* cheese), put them in the bottom of a pan, and cover them with corn bread batter. Bake and serve.

HOT DOGS SOUTHERN STYLE

Another corn bread special, known jocularly as a Scarlett O'Hot Dog.*

6 hot dogs	½ teaspoon salt
1 medium onion, diced	Orégano
½ cup diced celery	Thyme
½ cup diced green pepper	Corn bread batter
2 tablespoons butter	(see Corn Muffin Surprises)
8 ounces canned tomatoes	

Cut the hot dogs into coins. Cook them slowly, with the onion, the celery, and the green pepper in the butter. When the vegetables are tender, add the tomatoes and the seasonings. Simmer for 8–10 minutes. Pour into a casserole dish, cover with corn bread batter, and bake for 25 minutes at 400°. (Serves 4.)

Variations: More substantial vegetables—peas, carrots, corn—pleasantly alter this recipe. (By the way, leftover corn bread batter, should you have any, can always be made into muffins.)

* She, of course, was the heroine of the Civil War classic Dog-Gone with the Wind.

DILLY DOGS

The name of this number came up in a slightly hysterical conversation. Happily, it tasted good.

> 8 hot dogs
> 2 teaspoons dill
> 8 ounces sour cream

Slice the hot dogs in half lengthwise. Using half of the pieces, cover the bottom of a casserole. Sprinkle 1 teaspoon of dill on top of the dogs and cover them with 4 ounces of sour cream. Then make a second layer of hot dogs, dill, and sour cream. Bake for 15 minutes at 350°. (Serves 4.)

Variations: Chunks of Cheddar cheese are pure dynamite mixed in with the dogs. Also mix in some diced onion or olives.

DOG FRITTERS

These are good for any light meal. Serve them with a meat gravy (made, say, from an instant gravy mix). Incidentally, the French are very big on fritters, except that they call them *beignets*. A rose by any other name . . .

4 hot dogs	1 teaspoon baking powder
½ cup milk	¼ teaspoon salt
2 eggs	Gravy
1 cup flour	

Grate the hot dogs. Beat the milk and the eggs together. Add the hot dogs, the flour, the baking powder, and the salt. Stir until the mixture is smooth.

Drop spoonfuls of the batter into a frying pan with ¼" of hot (but not smoking) fat or cooking oil. Turn once. Drain and serve with gravy.

Variations: These make fine breakfast fare with maple syrup. Also, try making a cheese sauce (as in Macaroni, Cheese, and Dogs).

If they are cooked in a small amount of butter, they do not become as puffy.

SWEET-SOUR HOT DOGS

Here is a quick, tangy number good for both lunch and supper.

1 cup noodles
3 hot dogs
½ small onion
2–3 tablespoons butter
¼ cup ketchup
¼ cup vinegar
½ cup water
1 teaspoon sugar
¼ teaspoon paprika

Prepare the noodles according to the directions on the package and butter them with 1–2 tablespoons of the butter. Meanwhile, slice the hot dogs in half lengthwise. Then dice the onion and sauté it in the remaining butter for 5 minutes. Add the ketchup, the vinegar, the water, the sugar, and the paprika, and mix them over the fire. Next add the hot dogs and allow the mixture to simmer for another 5 minutes. Serve the sweet-sour hot dogs over or beside the buttered noodles. (Serves 2.)

Variations: You can substitute spaghetti (broken up before cooking), mashed potatoes, or rice for the noodles. Also, a little diced pineapple is good in the sauce, if you have it.

RUSSIAN WOLFHOUNDS

The dish is rather spicy and not recommended for faint stomachs. The sauce resembles Russian dressing—thus, the name.

½ small onion	2 tablespoons sour cream
¼ green pepper	1 tablespoon mayonnaise
Butter	1 tablespoon cocktail sauce
4 hot dogs	1 teaspoon water

Dice the onion and the green pepper, and sauté them in butter until the onion starts to brown. Slice the hot dogs in half lengthwise and then in half across their short axes. Mix the sour cream, the mayonnaise, the cocktail sauce, and the water.

Lay the dogs in a baking dish, cover them with the onion and green pepper, and pour the sauce over them. Bake for 15 minutes at 300°. (Serves 2.)

Variations: The main variations occur in the sauce. Ketchup and horseradish can be substituted for the cocktail sauce. Or you can leave the sauce out altogether, for a milder dish.

HOT DOG BUTTERFLIES, FLOWERS, AND OTHER BAROQUE DECORATIONS

Dressing up dinner plates with hot dogs is not recommended for grave and stately occasions. However, if a bit of levity seems appropriate, baroque hot dog decorations may spice up the meal. When hot dogs are cut in half lengthwise, covered, and heated, they curl; on this principle rests the basis of hot dog aesthetics.

Cut a hot dog in half. Then carefully begin cutting one of the pieces lengthwise in half, but cut only halfway down the piece. The result should be vaguely analogous to a tuning fork, split at one end, whole at the other. If you heat the piece, the split ends will curl away from each other and form a "butterfly."

You can make a "flower" out of the other piece by preparing it as you did the first and then carefully quartering the split halves. When heated, the four petals spring open wide.

Other decorating possibilities are "bow ties" (whole hot dogs with butterflies at each end) and "dumbbells" (whole hot dogs with flowers at each end). At last, a new art form—hot dog sculpture—is appearing on the horizon.

The decorations themselves can be served on top of mashed potatoes (flower beds?), in salads, or alone. They also make good hors d'oeuvres. They may be further decorated; pieces of pimento, for instance, can fit into the centers of the flowers. Beyond these suggestions, the reader must fend for himself. After all, techniques of art may be taught, but creativity stems directly from the artist.

DINNERS

If lunches are light meals, dinners are hearty ones. They ought to contain at least three elements: meat, starch, and vegetable. A recipe containing two hot dogs, one cup of starchy food (potato, rice, noodles, bread), and one cup of vegetables or salad per person, is probably sufficient in itself. Otherwise, you should supplement it. Open a can or package of vegetables or make a salad to compensate for a vegetable deficiency. For a starchy one, serve rolls or bread.

BAKED DOGS AND CREAMED TATERS

This entree goes well with peas or green beans. It looks great and thus makes good and cheap tête-à-tête fare.

> 4 hot dogs
> 2 medium potatoes (boiled)
> 3 tablespoons butter
> 1 tablespoon flour
> 1 cup heavy cream
> Salt and pepper
> Paprika

Cut the hot dogs lengthwise in half, and slice the potatoes. Lay the potato slices in a flat casserole dish and cover them with the hot dog strips.

In a saucepan, melt the butter and mix in the flour and the cream. Pour this over the dogs and taters. Season well and bake for 15 minutes at 350°. (Serves 2.)

Variations: You can get away with less than heavy cream. In fact, the meal will come off with milk, although you may need a bit more flour to thicken the sauce. If you don't have a casserole dish, you may cook this in a covered frying pan over a low fire for 20 minutes.

CREAMED AND CRISPY DOGS

The toss-together nature of preparing this dish makes it easy to control. You can keep it warm in the oven for hours until everyone is ready to eat.

    6 slices bacon
    6 hot dogs
    1 medium onion
    2 medium potatoes (boiled)
    1 can cream of mushroom soup
    8-ounce can diced carrots

Cook the bacon, saving the drippings, and lay it on a paper towel to drain. Cut the hot dogs into long, thin strips and then in half; dice the onion; and put both ingredients into the drippings-filled frying pan. Sauté them until the onion starts to brown. Drain off the drippings.

Chop up the potatoes and add them, with the soup and the carrots (including the carrots' liquid), to the pan. Cover and simmer for 10–15 minutes. Pour the mixture into a serving dish, topping with crumbled bacon. (Serves 4.)

Variations: Use any other creamed soup (cream of celery, for instance). Many other vegetables will work here as well. If the vegetables are fresh-cooked, be sure to include about ¼ cup of the cooking stock (the liquid in which they were cooked).

YAMMY HOT DOG BAKE

The easy way is to remember that yams come canned.

    4–6 hot dogs
    4 servings yams or sweet potatoes
    3 tablespoons butter
    Marshmallows

Slice the hot dogs in half lengthwise. Mash the yams, combining them with the butter. Then turn them into a shallow baking dish. Cover them with hot dogs and marshmallows. Bake at 300° for about 15 minutes until the marshmallows are golden brown. (Serves 4.)

Variations: You can add dates or crushed pineapple.

This recipe will work for squash as well, with or without the marshmallows. If you try it without them, add a tablespoon of prepared mustard.

IRISH SETTER STEW

Set her in the oven and let her go!

4–6 hot dogs	1 bay leaf
1 large potato	Parsley
1 large onion	Thyme
2–3 carrots	Salt and pepper
1 can chicken broth	

Cut the hot dogs into 1-inch chunks. Peel and slice the potato, the onion, and the carrots. Place these ingredients in a casserole and cover them with the chicken broth. Add the seasonings. Bake at 350° for about 1 hour. (Serves 4.)

Variations: This can also be stewed on top of the stove about the same length of time. Add some white wine after three-quarters of an hour for a pleasant surprise.

QUICK HOT DOG STEW

A good way to feed any number of people and get rid of leftovers at the same time. Almost anything will go into a stew. Furthermore, a stew is improved by aging: make it today for tomorrow's guests.

6 hot dogs	8-ounce can mixed vegetables
1 medium onion	1 can beef consommé
2 medium potatoes (boiled)	(undiluted)
8-ounce can diced carrots	Salt and pepper

Cut the hot dogs, the onion, and the potatoes into chunks. Drain the vegetables. Put all the ingredients in a saucepan, cover, and simmer for 15 minutes. (Serves 4.)

Variations: Instead of canned vegetables, try frozen or fresh-cooked ones. Also, instead of consommé, you can try other sauces, such as the instant gravy mixes available, or creamed soups.

SCALLOPED DOGATOES

This recipe is the gift of a young lady named Martha Holden, and the following one comes from her sister, Sally. Tasty, both of them. The recipes aren't bad either.

6 hot dogs	1 cup milk
2 large potatoes	1 cup grated cheese
2 medium onions	Salt and pepper
3 eggs	

Slice the hot dogs into thin coins, and the potatoes into thin pieces. Dice the onions. Grease the casserole, and put in a layer of potatoes, a layer of hot dog, a layer of onion, etc. ending at last with potatoes. Beat the eggs until very frothy; and add the milk, most of the grated cheese, the salt, and the pepper. Pour this mixture over the layers.

Sprinkle the rest of the grated cheese over the top, and bake uncovered for 45–55 minutes at 350° until almost solid. (Serves 4.)

Variation: This dish is great with diced green peppers mixed in with the onion.

HOT DOG CREOLE

The following recipe admits to a great deal of improvisation. Incidentally, stewed tomatoes are cooked with green peppers and onions already mixed in.

- 4–5 hot dogs
- 3 tablespoons butter
- 16-ounce can stewed tomatoes
- 6-ounce package Spanish rice
- Salt and pepper
- Paprika
- Chili pepper if desired (some like it hot)

Cut the hot dogs into small pieces and sauté them in the butter. Add and heat the tomatoes. Prepare the rice and drain it. Add it to the hot dog-tomato mixture, season, and mix well.

Either cover the rice and simmer over a low flame for 10

minutes, or place it in a casserole and bake for 5 minutes at 300°. (Serves 4.)

Variations: If you use Minute Rice's Spanish, the directions tell you to cook the rice in a sauce; afterward, simply add the hot dog-tomato mixture as above. You can use any regular rice and/or any type of cooked tomatoes; if you do, however, you will have to sauté some extra diced onion and green peppers with the hot dogs. Also, corn off the cob is very good in this dish.

DOG PILAFF

If you use a precooked rice, the cooking time is more than halved. Be sure to read the directions on the package.

4–6 hot dogs
1 small onion
2 tablespoons cooking oil
1 cup rice
2 beef bouillon cubes
Salt

Cut the hot dogs into chunks and dice the onion. Using the cooking oil, brown them and the rice slowly in a frying pan. Add water to 1″ above the level of the rice, and then add the bouillon cubes. Cover and simmer for 20–25 minutes (10 minutes with precooked rice). Season to taste. (Serves 4.)

Variations: Tomatoes, celery, and green pepper are good in this dish. For seasoning variations, try curry powder or chopped garlic.

DOGSTICK RICE CASSEROLE

An extremely adaptable dish, which, with a salad and rolls, makes an easy dinner party a possibility.

> 6 hot dogs
> 1 package Minute Rice Drumstick Mix
> 8-ounce can peas
> 1 can cream of mushroom soup

Cut the hot dogs into chunks, and prepare the rice according to the directions on the package. Place the hot dogs, the rice, the peas (including the stock), and the soup into a casserole dish. Cover and bake for 25–35 minutes at 350°. (Serves 4.)

Variations: This recipe is the foundation for a vast number of variations by using other vegetables, other creamed soups, and other rices.

STUFFED PEPPERS

Here, grated hot dogs work well in place of ground beef. If preparing rice presents problems, don't forget Minute Rice, which is a snap to get ready.

4 green peppers	Salt and pepper
2 hot dogs	Thyme
1 small onion	Paprika
2 cups boiled rice	2 slices American cheese
3 tablespoons butter	

Remove the seeds and core from the peppers and boil them for 5 minutes until tender. Meanwhile, grate the hot dogs and dice the onion. Sauté the boiled rice, the hot dogs, and the onion in the butter until the onion is light brown. Add the spices.

Fill the pepper shells with the mixture. Cover the top of each pepper with cheese, and broil them for 3–5 minutes. (Serves 2.)

Variations: I haven't had much success with stuffed peppers that don't contain rice, so I can't personally endorse nonrice experimentation. However, there are many different kinds of rice available in packaged form, some of which are interesting indeed.

CURRIED HOT DOGS

Curry is a distinctive spice from India and the East. For this recipe and the following one I am indebted to my lovely curry expert, Maya Chatterjee.

4 hot dogs	1 cup milk
1 small onion	Salt and pepper
2 tablespoons butter	4 cups cooked rice
1 teaspoon curry powder	Chutney

Dice the hot dogs and the onion, and sauté them in the butter. Add the curry powder, milk, salt and pepper. Cook over a low fire, stirring until the mixture thickens into a saucelike consistency. Serve over the rice with the chutney. (Serves 4.)

Variations: You can sauté green peppers with the onions. Also, try adding raisins with the milk. If you don't have any rice, try noodles, or, in real desperation, toast.

CURRIED HOT DOG CASSEROLE

Here is curry with the advantage of a casserole—it can be kept warm to be served later. Don't push this virtue, however.

- 4 hot dogs
- 1 tomato
- 1 small onion
- ½ green pepper
- ¼ cup raisins
- 2 tablespoons butter
- ½ teaspoon salt
- 1 teaspoon curry powder
- 4 cups cooked rice

Dice the hot dogs, the tomato, the onion, and the green pepper. Place them, together with the rest of the ingredients, into a casserole. Cover and bake for 25 minutes at 325°. The rice should not be allowed to dry out, so if you have to hold the dish in a warm oven for any length of time, add a couple of tablespoons of water. No single vegetable here is absolutely essential to the recipe.

FAT DOG CASSEROLE

Unless you can find a low-calorie cream cheese, here is an extremely fattening dish. Like all fattening dishes, it is also good.

- 8 hot dogs
- 1 tablespoon butter
- 8-ounce can tomato sauce
- ½ teaspoon garlic powder
- 1 teaspoon sugar
- ½ teaspoon salt
- 2 cups cooked noodles
- 4-ounce package cream cheese
- ½ cup sour cream
- ½ cup grated Cheddar cheese

Cut the hot dogs in half-inch chunks. In a skillet, heat them, along with the butter, the tomato sauce, the garlic powder, the sugar, and the salt over a medium fire.

Place the noodles in a greased casserole dish. Mix the cream cheese and the sour cream together with a fork, and spoon the mixture over the noodles. Add the hot dogs and the tomato sauce. Finally, sprinkle the top with the grated cheese, and bake for 30 minutes at 350°. (Serves 4.)

Variations: There are 2 levels to this casserole, and variations can occur at each level. Serve recipes like Curried Hot Dog Casserole or Hot Dog Creole over the creamed noodles. Or serve the hot dog-tomato sauce mixture over other noodle products, rice, or even mashed potatoes.

HOT DOODLES

This dish, contributed by my sister, is an easy way to feed a lot of people. The sauce in the recipe below can stretch from two to four servings, depending on the amount of noodles you make. Remember, one cup dry noodles equals about two cooked.

>3–4 hot dogs
>Butter
>1 can cream of chicken soup
>1 cup sour cream
>2 cups cooked noodles

Cut the dogs into chunks and brown them in butter in a frying pan. Add the soup and the sour cream. Heat, mixing well. Finally, pour the mixture over the noodles, stir, and serve. (Serves 2.)

Variations: You can vary both the noodle product (macaroni, shells, spaghetti) and the creamed soup (mushroom, celery, tomato).

NOODLE FRANK CASSEROLE

A friend's family's favorite frank recipe.

4 hot dogs	4 cups cooked egg noodles
2 tablespoons butter	1 can cream of mushroom soup
¼ cup diced onion	
¼ cup diced green pepper	1 cup warm water

Cut the hot dogs into coins. In the butter, sauté the hot dogs, the onion, and the green pepper. Place these ingredients in a casserole and add the noodles, the soup and the water. Mix everything. Top the casserole with:

> 1 cup soft bread crumbs
> 2 tablespoons melted butter
> 2 tablespoons grated Parmesan cheese

Bake for 30 minutes at 350°. (Serves 4.)

Variations: You may quite easily use other creamed soups and other pasta products.

HOT DOG SPAGHETTI

Don't worry about how much spaghetti to cook. If the package serves six and you want to serve two, just take somewhat less than half. Spaghetti stretches and contracts.

    6 hot dogs   1 teaspoon orégano
    1 large onion   Salt and pepper
    1 clove garlic   4 servings spaghetti
    3 tablespoons cooking oil   Grated Parmesan cheese
    1 can tomato paste

Make the sauce before the spaghetti, since the latter only takes about 10 minutes and can't be left sitting. Grate the hot dogs, and dice the onion, and mince the garlic. Sauté these ingredients in the cooking oil for 15 minutes. Add the tomato paste, the orégano, and the salt and pepper; cover; and simmer for 10–15 minutes more.

Cook the spaghetti. Either pour the sauce over each serving, or mix it up with the spaghetti all at once. Serve with the Parmesan cheese.

Variations: You can add lots of things to the sauce: mushrooms, green peppers, olives, or cheese for example. Also, you can use other noodles and this sauce to make casseroles.

SKEWERED HOT DOGS

A skewer is a long, thin pin with a loop at the head. Crammed with alternating foods, they make an interesting and attractive meal. Plan on two skewerfuls per person.

4 hot dogs	8 large stuffed olives
2 medium onions	2 tablespoons butter
8-ounce can pineapple chunks	¼ cup vinegar
	2 tablespoons brown sugar

Cut the hot dogs and the onions into chunks. Then thread the hot dog, onion, pineapple chunks, and the olives onto 4 skewers, alternating the ingredients (for aesthetic purposes).

Place the butter, the vinegar, and the brown sugar into the bottom of a bread pan; and heat in the oven until the butter melts. Place the skewers over the bread pan and bake them for 15–20 minutes at 350°. Turn them 2 or 3 times, basting them with the butter-vinegar mixture. (Serves 2.)

Variations: These can be cooked over an outdoor grill easily. Turn and baste as usual.

Other ingredients are definitely possible. Pickles, cucumbers, chunks of cheese, celery, and firm tomatoes are all good.

HOT DOG PAISANO

"When in Rome . . ."

4 hot dogs	6-ounce can tomato paste
1 medium zucchini	½ teaspoon garlic powder
1 small onion	½ teaspoon salt
1 tablespoon olive oil	Pepper
½ cup grated Parmesan cheese	

Cut the hot dogs into 1-inch chunks. Trim off the ends of the zucchini, and slice it. Dice the onion. Cook, covered, the zucchini and the onion in the olive oil over low heat for 10 or 15 minutes.

Add the hot dogs, 1/4 cup of cheese, the tomato paste, and the seasonings to the zucchini and the onion. Mix well. Turn into a casserole, sprinkle with the rest of the cheese, and bake for 20 minutes at 350°. (Serves 4.)

Variation: Summer squash may be substituted for the zucchini.

HOT DOG ROCKEFELLER

An excellent meal that should make everyone happy.

4 hot dogs	1/2 cup bread crumbs or crushed crackers
1 small onion	
1 package frozen spinach	Salt
1/2 cup sour cream	1/4 cup grated Parmesan cheese
1/2 cup butter	

Cut the hot dogs into 1-inch chunks, and dice the onion. Slightly cook the spinach. While it is cooking, mix in the sour cream and the butter, allowing the latter to melt. Add the hot dogs, the onion, the bread crumbs, or crackers and the salt.

Put the mixture into a baking dish and top it with the cheese. Bake it covered at 350° for 20 minutes. Uncover it, and bake for 10 minutes more. (Serves 2.)

Variations: Any type of greens (Swiss chard or beet greens, e.g.) will work fine. If they are fresh, they must be cooked longer initially (about 15 minutes), by dropping them into boiling water and reducing the fire to medium. Other vegetables in this recipe will create interesting dishes. If they are canned, they don't need much cooking. Sauté the onions in the butter; mix everything together as above; and bake for 15 minutes uncovered.

HOT DOG FLORENTINE

This recipe was contributed by one of my students, Robert Shute. I'm not sure of the derivation of its name, but it's so good that I am sure that Florence would be proud to claim it.

> 6–8 hot dogs
> 1 red cabbage
> 1 medium onion
> 3 tablespoons olive oil
> 1 clove garlic
> 1/3 cup burgundy

Slice the hot dogs in half lengthwise, and wash and quarter the cabbage. Boil the cabbage in about 2 inches of water for 20 minutes. Meanwhile, dice the onion and, using a large frying pan, sauté it in the olive oil. Remove the onion and drain it, saving the oil. Now, crush the garlic into the oil, add the hot dogs, and sauté them for 5 minutes. Remove the hot dogs, again saving the oil. Place the cabbage and the onion in the frying pan. Lay the hot dogs over the top. Pour in the burgundy, cover, and simmer for 15 minutes over low heat. Serve hot from the frying pan. (Serves 4.)

Variations: Robert was not anxious to have his recipe tampered with, but green cabbage, vegetable oil, and powdered garlic strike me as permissible substitutes. A slice or two of mozzarella cheese melted over the top is fantastic.

DIVINE DOGS

A canine version of one of my mother's favorite recipes.

- 8 hot dogs
- 1 package frozen broccoli (thawed)
- 4 tablespoons butter
- 4 tablespoons flour
- 1 can chicken broth
- ½ cup heavy cream
- ½ teaspoon Worcestershire sauce
- ½ cup grated Cheddar cheese
- 1 teaspoon prepared mustard
- 1 tablespoon sherry
- ½ teaspoon salt
- ¼ teaspoon pepper

Slice the hot dogs lengthwise in half. Place the broccoli in a casserole and cover it with the hot dog halves.

Melt the butter in a saucepan. Gradually add the flour, blending smoothly. Slowly add the chicken broth. Add the remaining ingredients. Stir until the cheese melts. Pour the sauce over the dogs. Bake at 400° for 20–25 minutes. Before serving, slosh a bit more sherry over the top. (Serves 4.)

Variation: This is also excellent with asparagus.

HOT DOG LOAF

> "A Book of Verses underneath the Bough,
> A Jug of Wine, a Loaf of Dog—and Thou"?

4 hot dogs	1 egg
2 medium potatoes (boiled)	½ teaspoon salt
1 small onion	1 tablespoon butter
¼ green pepper	2 slices American cheese

Grate the hot dogs and the potatoes into a mixing bowl. Dice and add the onion and the green pepper. Add the egg and the salt, and mix the whole thoroughly.

Press the mixture into a greased casserole, and dot the top with butter. Bake for 20 minutes at 300°. Then remove it from the oven, cover the top with cheese, return it to the oven, and bake it for 5 more minutes. (Serves 2.)

Variations: Aside from using different kinds of cheese, you can spread ketchup over the top with the butter. A half cup of diced apple makes the loaf more moist.

HOT DOGS AND SAUERKRAUT IN BEER

Gesundheit!

1 medium onion	1-pound can sauerkraut
2 tablespoons butter	6 ounces beer (drink the rest)
4 hot dogs	

Slice the onion and sauté it in the butter until the onion starts to brown. Add the hot dogs, the sauerkraut, and the beer; simmer for 10–15 minutes. (Serves 2.)

Variations: By leaving out the sauerkraut, this recipe becomes hot dogs cooked in beer. Serve them on buns, garnished with the onion.

A second variation, which I mention dutifully but not enthusiastically, involves the omission of the beer. To sparkle the resulting meal up a bit, add ½ teaspoon mustard seed and 1 tablespoon brown sugar.

SAUER BEAN HOT DOG CASSEROLE

Here is the sauer with something other than kraut.

6–8 hot dogs	½ teaspoon salt
3 medium potatoes	½ teaspoon pepper
1 tablespoon cooking oil	10-ounce can cut green beans
3 tablespoons white vinegar	

Cut the hot dogs in half lengthwise. Peel and slice the potatoes; then boil them for 10 minutes. Put the cooking oil, the vinegar, the salt, and the pepper into a casserole dish. Next, add the beans, along with ¼ cup of the stock (the water in the can). Cover the beans with the potatoes and top with the hot dogs. Bake, covered, for 30 minutes at 375°. (Serves 4.)

Variations: Carrots are good here in place of beans. Also, add Swiss cheese during the last 10 minutes of baking.

BAKED BEANS AND HOT DOGS

Baked beans and hot dogs, with coleslaw and brown bread, is as traditional in Maine on Saturday nights as baths. My mother's recipe follows. The leftover beans, by the way, are excellent warmed up for Sunday breakfast.

 4 hot dogs
 1 small onion
 2 tablespoons molasses
 2 tablespoons vinegar
 16-ounce can pea beans
 (without tomato sauce)

Cut the hot dogs in half lengthwise, and peel the onion. Mix the molasses and the vinegar with the beans and place them in a casserole dish. Poke the onion into the middle of the beans. Lay the hot dog halves over the top.

Cover, and bake the beans for 30 minutes at 325° or (and this is preferable) for 1 hour at 250°.

Variations: You can try kidney beans, which are large and mealy, or yellow-eyed. If you like tomato flavoring, try the tomato. Since many brands of beans already contain molasses, you often can get away without adding more. As a final suggestion, you might try browning the hot dog halves before baking them.

DAMBURGERS

The name, as I'm sure everyone has guessed by now, is a result of combining "dog" and "ham." The only other possibility was "hogburgers"—clearly unacceptable.

2 hot dogs
1 small onion
½ pound ground beef
¼ cup bread crumbs or
    crushed crackers

1 egg
Salt and pepper

Grate the hot dogs and dice the onion. Mix thoroughly the hot dogs, the onion, the ground beef, the bread crumbs or crackers, and the egg, working the ingredients together with your hands. Form the mixture into thick patties; then salt and pepper them.

Broil the patties until brown or place them in a frying pan, cover, and cook over a medium flame, turning once. (Makes 3–4 patties.)

Variations: An excellent addition to these ingredients is chopped green pepper. Also, do not overlook the possibility of dam-cheeseburgers. If you do not have bread crumbs or crackers, crumble some cereal (e.g., cornflakes or Wheaties.)

SPECIALTY DISHES

Into this section fall recipes that don't quite fit the criteria outlined in the Preface. Some of them—the soufflé and the pie, e.g.—are difficult to make. Others take a lot of time or require special ingredients. All, however, seemed to belong in this book.

MRS. SEARLES'S TEN IN ONE

Named "Ten in One" because of the number of ingredients (salt and pepper count separately), this recipe was given me by a date's mother, who was entranced by the idea of a male cookbooker. This meal makes very good leftovers.

4 hot dogs	1 cup onion rings
½ pound ground beef	1 cup sliced cabbage
1 tablespoon shortening	½ cup·ketchup
1 package French style green beans	½ cup water
	Salt and pepper

Slice the hot dogs and place them, with the ground beef and the shortening, into a casserole dish or a deep frying pan. Cover the meat first with the beans, then with the onion rings, and finally with the cabbage. Pour the ketchup and the water over the whole, and salt and pepper it.

Bake in a covered casserole at 275° for 45 minutes or cover and cook over a slow fire for 30 minutes without stirring. (Serves 4.)

HOT MANDARIN GINGER DOGS

Reminiscent of exotic Asia, this dish is sometimes known as Marco's Polo Ponies.

6–8 hot dogs	1 can mandarin orange sections
¼ cup orange juice	¾ cup sour cream
½ teaspoon salt	
1 teaspoon ground ginger	

Slice the hot dogs in half lengthwise, and lay them in a frying pan. Pour in the orange juice, and sprinkle the dogs with the salt and the ginger. Then cover them with the orange sections. Simmer for 15 minutes. Remove the pan from the heat; pour the sour cream over the top; and broil for a couple of minutes. (Serves 4).

Variations: Try using pineapple instead of or in addition to the orange. Great without the sour cream, on rice.

HOT DOG FRUIT BAKE

Here is an exotic little dish that is gorgeous on the table. Use it for important evenings or for doubting Thomases, who hold the hot dog in scorn.

6–8 hot dogs	5–10 maraschino cherries
8-ounce can peach halves	3 tablespoons butter
8-ounce can pear halves	½ cup brown sugar
8-ounce can pineapple slices	1 teaspoon curry powder

Slice the hot dogs in half lengthwise, and lay them in a shallow baking dish. Drain well the peaches, the pears, the pineapples, and the cherries. Arrange them on top of the hot dogs. Melt the butter; add the brown sugar and curry; and spoon the mixture over the fruit. Bake at 325° for 45 minutes. (Serves 4.)

Variations: Other fruits can replace or supplement the ones here. Grapes, apples, or bananas are possible, for instance. Nuts (walnuts, almonds, etc.) are good. Finally, the spice can be changed. Cinnamon or ginger works fine. Use white sugar with them, however.

MARINATED HOT DOGS

This is a good way to use up hot dogs that are beginning to grow old. A *bouquet garni* may sound too exotic for this book, but it is actually quite simple. I understand that you can even buy one ready-made.

> 1 bouquet garni
> *(which contains parsley, thyme, bay leaf
> and optionally sweet marjoram, basil)*
> 4 hot dogs
> 2 cups dry sherry

To make the *bouquet garni*, put the herbs into a small bag made of cheesecloth or some other coarse-woven cloth. Tie the top. Then put it, along with the hot dogs and the sherry, into a dish and marinate, or soak, them for 2–3 hours. You can, if you're strapped for time, score the hot dogs and get results under half an hour.

Then cook the hot dogs over charcoal or, if this is not possible, in a frying pan with a small amount of butter. Because the taste is very subtle, try to serve them without condiments.

Variations: Before marinating, cut the dogs into chunks. Then either serve them fried on top of rice or in Skewered Hot Dogs.

HOT DOG MOLD

You can use anything for a mold, including coffee cups for individual servings. Otherwise, all you need is time to get this ready.

- 7–8 hot dogs
- 8 large stuffed green olives
- 2 cans chicken broth
- 2 envelopes unflavored gelatin
- 3 tablespoons dried onion flakes or 1 small diced onion
- 1/4 cup lemon juice or vinegar
- 1/4 teaspoon pepper
- 16-ounce can diced carrots
- 16-ounce can French style green beans

Dice the hot dogs and the olives. In a large saucepan, slowly heat the chicken broth and the gelatin until the latter dissolves. Add the onion, the lemon juice or vinegar, and the pepper.

If you wish to be fancy, arrange some of the vegetables artistically on the bottom of the mold. Add the rest of the vegetables —olives, carrots, and beans—and the hot dogs to the hot broth mixture. Pour it into the mold, and chill it for at least 4 hours, preferably overnight. Do not freeze it.

To serve, run a knife around the edge of the gelatin. Then dip the mold very quickly in hot water. Covering the top with a platter, invert both. The mold can then be lifted from the plate, leaving the gelatin behind. Slice it and serve on lettuce with mayonnaise or with a sauce made from 1 part prepared mustard to 4 parts sour cream. (Makes 1½ quarts.)

Variations: The vegetables are variable and may be frozen or fresh-cooked.

TACO DOGS

You need taco shells for this one. They come in a package, ready to cook, yet they are storable for a long time. The sauce, as the ingredients suggest, is hot. Very hot.

 6 hot dogs
 16-ounce can chili beans or a 16-ounce can kidney beans with 2 tablespoons chili powder
 12 taco shells
 1 can shredded lettuce
 2 cups grated cheese

Grate the hot dogs and mash them together with the beans. Heat this mixture thoroughly in a frying pan. Prepare the taco shells according to the directions on the package. Put shredded lettuce at the bottom of the shell, the hot dog-bean mixture in the middle, and grated cheese sprinkled on the top.

Serve with hot sauce:

1 cup canned tomato sauce	¼ teaspoon sugar
1 tablespoon chili powder	½ teaspoon salt
2 teaspoons dry mustard or horseradish	¼ teaspoon pepper
1 teaspoon onion juice or ½ small onion, diced	

Heat and stir these ingredients in a saucepan. Pour the sauce very carefully over the tacos. (Serves 4.)

Variations: It is possible to mix all the hot ingredients into the beans, thus avoiding the sauce. If you do, however, individual control of the tacos' hotness becomes impossible. Remember that you can substitute hot dog rolls for the taco shells.

HOT DOG MANICOTTI

Manicotti shells are forms of pasta resembling sections of garden hose. They are cooked, stuffed, and baked.

> 4 hot dogs
> 1 medium onion
> ½ green pepper
> 2 tablespoons olive oil
> 1 clove garlic
> 8-ounce can tomato sauce
> Salt and pepper
> Orégano
> 4 manicotti shells
> 1 cup grated mozzarella cheese

Dice the hot dogs, the onion, and the green pepper. Sauté them in the olive oil, crushing and adding the clove of garlic. After 5 minutes, add half of the tomato sauce and the seasonings. Stir, cover, and simmer for 10 minutes.

Meanwhile, prepare the manicotti shells according to the directions on the package. Using a spoon, stuff the shells with the hot dog-tomato mixture. Place the stuffed shells in a baking dish. Pour the rest of the tomato sauce over them and cover with cheese. Bake at 350° for 25 minutes. (Serves 2.)

Variations: With the proper pasta shell, this filling can also be used to make lasagne. Experiment.

HOT DOG PIE

This will be the most complex recipe in this book. Accordingly, I have broken it down into its various operations, with commentary along the way. If you have trouble imagining what hot dog pie is like, think of a chicken pie with dogs instead of hens.

MRS. SAGAN'S PIECRUST

Mrs. Sagan cooked for my mother's family for years and left us her piecrust as a legacy. The recipe makes enough dough for two pies; and, for reasons not clear to the kitchen science, it doesn't work as well when cut in half. However, wrapped in wax paper, any leftover dough will keep at least three weeks in the refrigerator.

3 cups flour
1 teaspoon salt
3 tablespoons sugar
1 heaping cup shortening
Cold water

Sift the flour, the salt, and the sugar together. Cut in the shortening with a knife or a pastry cutter. Then add cold water a little at a time, until the dough holds together but is not sticky. (If you should go too far, shake in a bit of flour.)

Roll the dough thin on a floured pastry cloth, or, lacking that, on a tabletop previously sprinkled with flour. The flour prevents sticking. Invert a 9-inch pie pan on the dough, and cut a circle with a radius 2 inches larger or more than the pan. This will be the bottom of the pie. Lay it carefully into the pan, repairing any holes that develop, and shape it to the sides.

Variations: This is a great crust, but if you are strapped for time, alternatives abound. There are piecrust mixes available and also you can consider frozen pie shells, which can be found in many supermarkets. (If you use a frozen shell, of course, you won't have a top crust.)

PIE FILLING

2 tablespoons butter
1–2 tablespoons flour
1 cup milk or light cream
5–6 hot dogs
8-ounce can peas
8-ounce can diced carrots
Salt and pepper
Paprika

Melt the butter and blend in the flour. Then stir in the milk or cream. The mixture should be thick and creamy. Cut the hot dogs into inch-long chunks and add them, along with the vegetables, to the cream sauce. Finally, pour this into the pie shell, and season.

Variations: The vegetables in this pie are limited only by your taste and imagination. Bits of boiled potato, green or lima beans, asparagus, mushrooms, or tomato—all precooked—are possibilities. Just aim for about 2 cups of vegetables in all.

BAKING

Roll out a second crust. Wet the rim of the bottom crust with cold water on your finger. Then lay the second crust on top, trim the excess dough away, and press the edges with your finger or a fork. With a fork or knife, poke some holes in the crust. Bake at 450° for 5 minutes (to set the crust), and then cut back to 325° for 25 minutes.

SOUFFLE AUX CHIENS

The key to this number is organization. Lay out all the ingredients before you start to cook anything; once a soufflé gets rolling, it's hard to slow down.

1½ cups milk
3 tablespoons flour
1 teaspoon salt
Pepper
4 eggs
2 cups diced cheese
1 teaspoon Worcestershire sauce
2 hot dogs
8-ounce can sliced mushrooms

Put the milk, the flour, the salt, and the pepper into a large saucepan. Next separate the egg yolks from the whites (see Puffy Puppies). Put the whites into one mixing bowl and the yolks, the cheese, and the Worcestershire sauce into a second. Then dice the hot dogs and open the can of mushrooms. Finally, beat the egg whites until they are stiff, that is, until mounds of egg white hold their shapes.

Cover the saucepan containing the milk and simmer for 3–5 minutes, until the mixture is creamy. Then add, while still on the fire, the bowlful of yolks and cheese. Mix well. Next fold in the egg whites, and add the hot dogs and the mushrooms. Pour into a casserole and bake for 45–50 minutes at 300°. This soufflé holds very well (many tend to collapse quickly), but still, the sooner it is served, the better. (Serves 4.)

Variations: Many solid ingredients can be substituted for the mushrooms: pimentos, olives, onions, etc.

HOT DOG QUICHE

An elegant pie that, since it needs no top crust, may be made with a store-bought pie shell. If you are willing to go to the trouble, there is a piecrust recipe on the Hot Dog Pie page.

- 4 hot dogs
- 1 tablespoon butter
- 1 unbaked 9-inch pie shell
- 3 eggs
- 1½ cups heavy cream
- ½ cup grated Swiss cheese
- ½ teaspoon salt
- Pepper
- Nutmeg

Cut the hot dogs into coins, and sauté them in the butter until brown. Drain and spread them on the bottom of the pie shell. Beat the eggs slightly and stir in the cream, the cheese, and the seasonings. Pour the mixture into the shell over the hot dogs. Bake at 375° for 35–40 minutes, until the pie shell is brown and the filling is firm. (Serves 4.)

Variations: You may use other types of cheeses. The substitution of bacon for the hot dogs makes *quiche Lorraine*, the more usual form of *quiche*.

HOT DOGS A LA PAELLA

This recipe is a gift from a friend who teaches Spanish. She requests that it be pronounced "Pah-eh′-yah." (Incidentally, prepared packages of saffron rice are sold in most groceries.)

6 hot dogs	2 cups cooked rice
½ cup diced onion	A few pieces saffron
½ clove garlic, diced	½ cup canned, frozen, or
4–5 tablespoons olive oil	fresh-cooked peas

Cut the hot dogs into 1-inch pieces. Sauté them for 5 minutes, with the onion and the garlic, in the olive oil. Add the rice, the saffron, and the peas, mixing well. Cover and simmer the mixture over low heat for 15–20 minutes. (Serves 4.)

Variations: In Spain, *paella* contains many different meats, singly and in combination—sausage, shrimp, chicken pieces, ham, etc. The dish itself may also be baked in a moderate oven (350°) for 15 minutes

Glossary of Terms

Bake — to cook in the oven by indirect heating.

Boil — to cook in boiling water (212°).

Broil — to cook directly exposed to the source of heat, either over charcoal or in an oven, on the top rack close to the heating coils. In many ovens, you should leave the door open while broiling.

Casserole — a fireproof baking dish, or any recipe baked in such a dish.

Chafing dish — a dish that sits over a portable source of heat, such as a candle.

Cut (shortening into flour) — to combine with downward strokes of a knife, fork, or pastry cutter.

Dice — to cut into small squares.

Fold — to combine beaten ingredients by carefully turning them down, so that the bubbles gained by beating are not lost.

Fry (deep fat) — to cook in ½" or more hot (not smoking) fat or cooking oil. When food is dropped in, the fat bubbles excitedly.

Grate, or more accurately with hot dogs, shred — to cut into bits using a metal sheet with holes punched in it.

Grill — with meat, to broil; with sandwiches, to brown with butter in a frying pan.

Marinate — to soak in a flavoring liquid.

Poach — to cook, uncovered, in steaming (not boiling) liquid on top of the stove.

Sauté — to cook in a small quantity of fat over a medium fire.

Simmer — to cook, covered, in steaming (not boiling) liquid on top of the stove.

Stock — the liquid in which something is cooked.

Appendix A: Grocery List

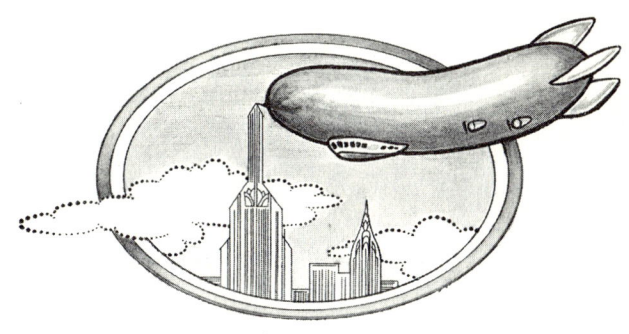

MEATS
   hot dogs   bacon   ground beef

BREADS
        bread   brown bread
        hot dog rolls   crescent rolls
        hamburger buns   taco shells

VEGETABLES, FRESH
   onions   tomatoes   lettuce
   cabbage   celery   radishes
   cucumber   green peppers   potatoes

VEGETABLES, CANNED OR FROZEN

green beans	diced carrots	yams
kidney beans	tomato paste	spinach
onion rings	corn	pea beans
peas	tomatoes	mushrooms
sauerkraut	olives	broccoli

DAIRY PRODUCE

eggs	butter	orange juice
American cheese	cream	cream cheese
milk	Cheddar cheese	Parmesan cheese
Swiss cheese	sour cream	

PASTA

- noodles
- spaghetti
- manicotti shells
- macaroni

STAPLES

flour	powdered sugar	baking powder
gelatin	sugar	bouillon cubes
crackers	olive oil	peanut butter
brown sugar	cornmeal	cornstarch
cooking oil	shortening	

(optional)

bread crumbs	pancake mix	biscuit mix

SOUPS

    beef bouillon   cream of chicken
    beef consommé   chicken broth
    cream of mushroom

FRUITS, FRESH

        apples   pineapples

FRUITS, CANNED

    pear halves   peach halves
    mandarin oranges   maraschino cherries
    pineapple chunks   pineapple slices

CONDIMENTS

mayonnaise	mustard	Worcestershire sauce
vinegar	chutney	jelly
honey	ketchup	barbecue sauce
horseradish	gravy mix	marshmallow
relish	jam	maple syrup
molasses	cocktail sauce	walnuts

SPICES

salt	dried onion flakes	paprika
chili powder	garlic salt	ginger
bay leaf	orégano	parsley
chives	pepper	saffron
thyme	curry powder	

APPENDIX A: GROCERY LIST

LIQUORS
burgundy   beer   sherry (dry)

Remember to buy small cans and small amounts of fresh perishables unless you're planning for a large group. If something won't keep, you must either eat it up or throw it out.

Appendix B: Utensil List

This list assumes you have eating utensils, a stove, and a can opener. Numbers and sizes, when needed, are given.

SMALL THINGS
    measuring spoons (set)
    measuring cup
    paring knife
    large chopping knife
        (a cutting board saves knives and counter tops)

spatula
skewers (4)
egg beater
grater
   (I like the box-shaped kind that has different sized holes on each side.)

POTS AND PANS

casserole, with cover (approx. 1½ quarts)
saucepans (2: ½ quart and 2 quarts)
frying pan, with cover
bread pan
muffin tin (for 12 muffins)
cookie sheet
mixing bowl (which can double as a salad bowl)
pie plate (9")

EXOTIC EQUIPMENT

rolling pin (you can use a bottle or a large jar)
chafing dish
fondue pot and paraphernalia

Index

"All meat" hot dogs, 1
American cheese, 13, 96
   doggie thins, 9
   eggs Benedogged (eggs Benedict), 23
   hot dog loaf, 76
   pizza puppy toasts, 39
   spud pups, 42
   stuffed peppers, 66–67
   stuffed potatoes, 43–44
Apple and hot dog cum cheese, 50–51
Asparagus
   divine dogs, 75

Bacon
   creamed and crispy dogs, 61
   hot dog potato gravy, 46
   stuffed dogs, 41–42
   sweet potato boats, 44–45
Bagel dogs, 29
   variations, 29
Bake, defined, 93
Baked beans and hot dogs, 78
Baked dogs and creamed taters, 60
Barbecued dogs, 37–38
   variations, 38
Battered bits, 10–11
   variations, 11
Beans
   baked, and hot dogs, 78
   chili dogs, 38–39
   green, sauer bean hot dog casserole, 77
   kidney
     and hot dogs, baked, 78
     taco dogs, 86–87
Beef, ground
   chili dogs, 38–39
   damburgers, 78–79
   Mrs. Searles's Ten in One, 82

Beer, hot dogs and sauerkraut in, 76–77
Biscuits, hot dog, 52–53
Boil, defined, 93
Bowser buns, 31–32
"Bow ties" (hot dog decorations), 58
Bread pudding, savory hot dog, 51–52
Breakfasts, 17–24
  eggs Benedogged (eggs Benedict), 22
  French toasted dog, 18
  hot dog crêpes, 23–24
  hot dog pancakes, 18–19
  hot dogs and shirred eggs, 22
  omelette au chien chaud, 19–20
  poached eggs on hot dog hash, 21
  scrambled dogs, 20
  soft-boiled eggs with creamed dogs, 21–22
Broil, defined, 93
Buns, bowser, 31–32
Butter, use of, 4, 96
"Butterflies" (hot dog decorations), 58

Cabbage
  hot dog Florentine, 74–75
  slaw, coledog, 33–34
Cabbage slaw, coledog, 33–34
Cape Cod cranberry dog salad, 37
Carrots, cooking time for, 5
Casings, 2
Casserole(s)
  curried hot dog, 68
  defined, 93
  dogstick rice, 66
  fat dog, 68–69
  macaroni, cheese, and dogs, 50
  Mrs. Searles's Ten in One, 82
  noodle frank, 70
  sauer bean hot dog, 77
Chatterjee, Maya, 67
Cheddar cheese
  dilly dogs, 55
  divine dogs, 75
  fat dog casserole, 68–69
  hot dog salad sandwich, 28
  and macaroni and dogs, 50
  omelette au chien chaud, 19–20
  savory hot dog bread pudding, 51–52

stuffed dogs, 41–42
Cheese
   bowser buns, 31–32
   hot dog and apple cum, 50–51
   hot dog paisano, 72–73
   and macaroni and dogs, 50
   peanut pup sandwiches, 28
   piglets in blankets, 8–9
   pizza puppy toasts, 39
   roll-ups, 12–13
   scalloped dogatoes, 63–64
   sloppy dog on a bun, 40
   soufflé au chiens, 90
   spud pups, 42–43
   stuffed tomatoes, 40–41
   See also specific kinds of cheese, e.g., American cheese; Cheddar cheese; Cream cheese; Parmesan cheese
Cheese, macaroni, and dogs, 50
Chianti wine, potted dogs in, 13
"Chicken dog," 1
Chili beans
   taco dogs, 86–87
Chili dogs, 38–39
Chipped dogs, creamed, 48
Chowder, Down-East hot dog, 30
Coledog slaw, 33–34
Condiments and spices, on grocery list, 97
Corn, cooking time for, 5
Corn, creamed, dogs and, 48
Cornmeal
   corn muffin surprises, 53–54
   hot dog pancakes, 18–19
   hot dogs Southern style, 54
Corn muffin surprises, 53–54
Cranberry dog salad, Cape Cod, 37
Cream cheese
   fat dog casserole, 68–69
   hot dog paté, 8
   pops, 12
   puffy puppies, 33
Cream cheese pops, 12
Creamed chipped dogs, 48–49
Creamed corn and dogs, 48
Creamed and crispy dogs, 60–61
Creamed dogs, soft-boiled eggs with, 21–22
Creamed taters and baked dogs, 60

Cream sauces
    red sour cream and onion, 16
    sour cream and horseradish, 15
Creole, hot dog, 64–65
Crêpes, hot dog, 23–24
    fillings, 24
    variations, 24
Crunchy hot dogs, 29
Currant dogs, 14
Curried hot dog casserole, 68
Curried hot dogs, 67
Cut (shortening into flour), defined, 94

Damburgers, 78–79
    variations, 79
Decorations, plate and table (hot dog "sculpture,") 58
Deviled eggs, dog, 10
Dice (dicing), defined, 94
Dilly dogs, 55
Dinners, 59–79
    baked beans and hot dogs, 78
    baked dogs and creamed taters, 60
    casseroles
        curried hot dog, 68
        dogstick rice, 66
        fat dog, 68–69
        noodle frank, 70
        sauer bean hot dog, 77
    creamed and crispy dogs, 60–61
    curried hot dog casserole, 68
    curried hot dogs, 67
    damburgers, 78–79
    divine dogs, 75
    dog pilaff, 65
    dogstick rice casserole, 66
    fat dog casserole, 68–69
    hot dog Creole, 64–65
    hot dog Florentine, 74–75
    hot dog loaf, 76
    hot dog paisano, 72–73
    hot dog Rockefeller, 74–75
    hot dog spaghetti, 71
    hot dogs and sauerkraut in beer, 76–77
    hot doodles, 68
    Irish setter stew, 62
    noodle frank casserole, 70
    quick hot dog stew, 63
    sauer bean hot dog casserole, 77
    scalloped dogatoes, 63–64

skewered hot dogs, 71–72
stews
    Irish setter, 62
    quick hot dog, 63
stuffed peppers, 66–67
yammy hot dog bake, 61–62
Divine dogs, 75
Dog-deviled eggs, 10
Dog fritters, 55–56
Doggie balls, 11
Doggie thins, 9
Dog in a foxhole, 45
Dog pilaff, 65
Dogstick rice casserole, 66
Down-East hot dog chowder, 30
"Dumbbells" (hot dog decorations), 58

Egg-dog soup, 30–31
Eggs
    battered bits, 10–11
    Benedogged (Benedict), 22
    dog-deviled, 10
    dog fritters, 55–56
    doggie balls, 11
    French toasted dogs, 18
    H.D. potato salad, 34–35
    hot dog crêpes, 23–24
    hot dog Newburg, 49
    hot dog pancakes, 19
    omelette au chien chaud, 19–20
    poached, on hot dog hash, 21
    puffy puppies, 33
    puppy pies, 32
    scalloped dogatoes, 63–64
    scrambled dogs, 20
    shirred, hot dogs and, 72
    soft-boiled, with creamed dogs, 21–22
    soufflé aux chiens, 90
    soups
        egg-dog, 30–31
    tossed salad, 36
    use of, 4, 96
Eggs Benedogged (eggs Benedict), 23
    variations, 23
Equipment. See Utensils and equipment
Extenders, use in hot dog manufacture of, 1

Fat dog casserole, 68–69
"Flowers" (hot dog decorations), 58
Fold, defined, 94

French toasted dog, 18
Fritters, dog, 55–56
Fruit(s)
    bake, hot dog, 83–84
    fresh and canned, on grocery list, 17
    hot dog and apple cum cheese, 50–51
    hot mandarin ginger dogs, 82–83
    yammy hot dog bake, 61–62
Fruit bake, hot dog, 83–84
Fry (deep fat), defined, 94

Gelatin. See Hot dog mold
Glossary of terms, 93–94
Grate (grating, shredding), 2, 26
    defined, 94
Gravy, hot dog potato, 46
Green beans
    cooking time for, 5
    sauer bean hot dog casserole, 77
Grill (grilling), defined, 94
Grocery list, 95–98
    breads, 96
    condiments and spices, 97
    dairy products, 96
    fruits, fresh and canned, 97
    liquors, 98
    meats, 94
    pasta, 96
    soups, 97
    staples, 96
    vegetables, canned or frozen, 96
Ground beef. See Beef, ground

Hash, hot dog, poached eggs on, 21
H.D. potato salad, 34–35
Holden, Martha, 63
Holden, Sally, 63
Hors d'oeuvres, 7–16
    battered bits, 10–11
    cream cheese pops, 12
    currant dogs, 14
    dog-deviled eggs, 10
    doggie balls, 11
    doggie thins, 9
    hot dog fondue, 15–16
    hot dog paté, 8
    piglets in blankets, 8–9
    pizza puppy toasts, 39
    potted dogs, 13
    sauced dogs, 14–15
    sauces for, 11, 13, 15–16
    Swiss cheese roll-ups, 12–13

Horseradish and sour cream sauce, 15
Hot dog and apple cum cheese, 51
Hot dog biscuits, 52–53
Hot dog bread pudding, savory, 51–52
Hot dog chowder, Down-East, 30
    variations, 30
Hot dog Creole, 64–65
Hot dog crêpes, 23–24
    fillings, 24
    variations, 24
Hot dog Florentine, 74–75
Hot dog fondue, 15–16
    sauces for, 15–16
Hot dog fruit bake, 83–84
    variations, 83–84
Hot dog loaf, 76
Hot dog macaroni salad, 35
    variations, 35
Hot dog manicotti, 87
Hot dog mold, 85
    variations, 85
Hot dog Newburg, 49
Hot dog paisano, 72–73
    variation, 73
Hot dog pancakes, 18–19
    variation, 19
Hot dog paté, 8
    variations, 8
Hot dog pie, 88–89
    baking, 89
    filling, 89
    piecrust, 88
Hot dog potato gravy, 46
    variations, 46
Hot dog quiche, 91
    variations, 91
Hot dog Rockefeller, 73–74
    variations, 73–74
Hot dogs
    "all meat," 1
    casings, 2
    "chicken dog," 1
    "extenders," 1
    forms, 2
    glossary of terms, 93–94
    grating or shredding, 2, 26, 94
    grocery list, 95–98
    hints and prefatory recipes, 3–5
    keeping (refrigerating), 2
    kinds and ingredients, 1–2
    selecting brands, 2
    "skinless," 2

spices and condiments, 2, 97
utensils and equipment, 99–100
Hot dogs, baked beans and, 78
Hot dogs, grated (shredded), 2, 26, 94
Hot dogs, marinated, 84
bouquet garni for, 84
variations, 84
Hot dogs, skewered, 71–72
Hot dog salad sandwich, 28
variations, 28
Hot dogs à la paella, 91–92
variations, 92
Hot dog sandwich(es), 26–29
bagel dogs, 29
bowser buns, 31–32
hot hot dog, 27
peanut pup, 27
salad, 28
stuffed dog on a bun, 40
See also Sandwich(es)
Hot dogs and sauerkraut in beer, 76–77
variations, 77
Hot dogs and shirred eggs, 22
variations, 22
Hot dog spaghetti, 71
variations, 71

Hot dogs Southern style, 54
variations, 54
Hot dog stew, quick, 63
Hot dog waggle, 47
variation, 47
Hot doodles, 69–70
variations, 70
Hot hot dog sandwiches, 27
variations, 27
Hot mandarin ginger dogs, 82–83
variations, 83
Hush puppies, 53

Irish setter stew, 62
variations, 62

Jelly
currant dogs, 14

Kidney beans
baked, and hot dogs, 78
taco dogs, 86–87

Lasagne, hot dog, 87
LeBlanc, Anne, 23
Liquors
on grocery list, 98

See also Wine(s); specific recipes
Loaf, hot dog, 76
Lunches, 25–58
   bagel dogs, 29
   barbecued dogs, 37–38
   bowser buns, 31–32
   Cape Cod cranberry dog salad, 37
   chili dogs, 38–39
   coledog slaw, 33–34
   corn muffin surprises, 53–54
   creamed chipped dogs, 48
   creamed corn and dogs, 48
   crunchy hot dogs, 29
   dilly dogs, 55
   dog in a foxhole, 45
   dog fritters, 55–56
   Down-East hot dog chowder, 30
   hot dog and apple cum cheese, 50–51
   hot dog biscuits, 52–53
   hot dog macaroni salad, 35
   hot dog Newburg, 49
   hot dog potato gravy, 46
   hot dogs, Southern style, 54
   hot dog salad sandwich, 28
   hot dog sandwiches, 26–29
   See also Sandwich(es)
   hot dog waggle, 47
   hot hot dog sandwiches, 27
   hush puppies, 53
   macaroni, cheese, and dogs, 50
   peanut pup sandwich, 27–28
   pizza puppy toasts, 39
   potato salad, H.D., 34–35
   puppy pies, 32
   Russian wolfhounds, 57
   salads
      Cape Cod cranberry dog, 37
      H.D. potato, 34–35
      hot dog macaroni, 35
      sandwiches, 28
      tossed, 36
   sandwiches, 26–29
   See also Sandwich(es)
   savory hot dog bread pudding, 51–52
   sheep dog's pie, 46–47
   slaw, coledog, 33–34
   sloppy dog on a bun, 40
   spud pups, 42–43
   stuffed dogs, 41–42
   stuffed tomatoes, 40–41
   sweet potato boats, 44–45

sweet-sour hot dogs, 56–57
tossed salad, 36

Macaroni, cheese, and dogs, 50
   variations, 50
Macaroni salad, hot dog, 35
   variations, 35
Mandarin (orange) ginger dogs, hot, 82–83
Manicotti, hot dog, 87
   variations, 87
Margarine, use of, 4
Marinate, defined, 94
Marinated hot dogs, 84
   bouquet garni for, 84
   variations, 84
Mrs. Sagan's piecrust, 88
Mrs. Searles's Ten in One, 82
Mold, hot dog, 85
Mushrooms, 96
   soufflé aux chiens, 90

Newburg, hot dog, 49
Noodle(s), 96
   fat dog casserole, 68–69
   frank casserole, 70
   hot dog salad, 35
   hot doodles, 69–70
   sweet-sour hot dogs, 56–57
Noodle frank casserole, 70
   variations, 70

Olives, 96
   cream cheese pops, 12
   doggie thins, 9
   skewered hot dogs, 71–72
   stuffed dogs, 41–42
   tossed salad, 36
Omelets, 20
   omelette au chien chaud, 19–20
Omelette au chien chaud, 19–20
   variations, 20
Onion and red sour cream sauce, 16
Onions, use of, 4
Orange(s), 97
   hot mandarin ginger dogs, 82–83
Ovens, 3–4
   preheating, 4

Paella, hot dogs à la, 91–92
Pancakes, hot dog, 18–19
   variation, 19

Pans. See Pots and pans, on utensil list
Parmesan cheese, 96
   hot dog paisano, 72–73
   hot dog Rockefeller, 73–74
   hot dog spaghetti, 71
Paté, hot dog, 8
Peanut butter and hot dog sandwich, 27–28
Peanut pup sandwich, 27–28
   variations, 28
Peas, 96
   cooking time for, 5
   hot dog waggle, 47
Peppers, stuffed, 66–67
Pie(s)
   baking, 89
   filling, 89
   hot dog, 88–89
   hot dog quiche, 91
   piecrust, 88
   puppy, 32
Piecrust, Mrs. Sagan's, 88
Piglets in blankets, 8–9
   variations, 9
Pizza puppy toasts, 39
   variations, 39
Poach, defined, 94
"Poached" eggs, 4

Poached eggs on hot dog hash, 21
   variations, 21
Potato(es), 4–5, 95
   boats, sweet, 44–45
   bowser buns, 31–32
   creamed, baked dogs and, 60
   dog in a foxhole, 45
   gravy, hot dog, 46
   hot dog loaf, 76
   Irish setter stew, 62
   puffy puppies, 33
   quick hot dog stew, 63
   salad, H.D., 34–35
   scalloped dogatoes, 63–64
   sheep dog's pie, 46–47
   spud pups, 42–43
   stuffed, 43–44
   sweet
      boats, 44–45
      hot dog bake, 61–62
Potato boats, sweet, 44–45
   variations, 45
Potato salad, H.D., 34–35
   variations, 35
Pots and pans, on utensil list, 100
Potted dogs, 13

variations, 13
Pudding(s)
  bread, savory hot dog, 51–52
Puffy puppies, 33
Puppy pies, 32
  variations, 32

Quiche, hot dog, 91
Quick hot dog stew, 63
  variations, 63

Red cabbage
  hot dog Florentine, 74–75
Red sour cream and onion sauce, 16
Rice
  dog pilaff, 65
  dogstick casserole, 66
  hot dog Creole, 64–65
  hot dogs à la paella, 91–92
  stuffed peppers, 66–67
Rice casserole, dogstick, 66
Roll-ups, Swiss cheese, 12–13
Russian wolfhounds, 57
  variations, 57

Saffron rice
  hot dogs à la paella, 91–92

Salad(s)
  Cape Cod cranberry dog, 37
  hot dog macaroni, 35
  H.D. potato, 34–35
  sandwich, hot dog, 28
  tossed, 36
Sandwich, John Montagu, fourth Earl of, 26
Sandwich(es)
  bagel dogs, 29
  barbecued dogs, 37–38
  bowser buns, 31–32
  chili dogs, 38–39
  crunchy hot dogs, 29
  hot dog, 26–29
  hot dog paté, mixture for, 8
  hot hot dog, 27
  peanut pup, 27–28
  sloppy dog on a bun, 40
  See also Hot dog sandwich(es)
Sauced dogs, 14–15
  variations, 15
Sauces
  barbecued dogs, 37–38
  cocktail, Russian wolfhounds, 57
  dilly dogs, 55
  dog fritters, 56

hot, taco dogs, 86
hot dog fondue, 15–16
macaroni, cheese, and dogs, 50
red sour cream and onion, 16
sauced dogs, 14–15
sour cream and horseradish, 15
sweet-sour hot dogs, 56–57
Sauer bean hot dog casserole, 77
variations, 77
Sauerkraut and hot dogs in beer, 76–77
Sauté, defined, 94
Savory hot dog bread pudding, 51–52
variations, 52
Scalloped dogatoes, 63–64
variations, 64
Scrambled dogs, 20
variations, 20
"Sculpture" (decorations), hot dog, 58
Sheep dog's pie, 46–47
variations, 47
Shirred eggs and hot dogs, 22
variations, 22
Shute, Robert, 74, 75
Simmer, defined, 94
Skewered hot dogs, 71–72
variations, 72
Slaw, coledog, 33–34
variations, 34
Sloppy dog on a bun, 40
variations, 40
Soft-boiled eggs with creamed dogs, 21–22
variations, 22
Soufflé aux chiens, 90
variations, 90
Soups, 30–31
Down-East hot dog chowder, 30
egg-dog, 30–31
on grocery list, 96
Sour cream, red, and onion sauce, 16
Sour cream and horseradish sauce, 15
Sour-sweet hot dogs, 56–57
variations, 57
Southern style hot dogs, 54
Spaghetti, hot dog, 71
Specialty dishes, 81–92
hot dog fruit bake, 83–84

hot dog manicotti, 87
hot dog mold, 85
hot dog pie, 88–89
hot dog quiche, 91
hot dogs à la paella, 91–92
hot mandarin ginger dogs, 82–83
marinated hot dogs, 84
Mrs. Searles's Ten in One, 82
soufflé aux chiens, 90
taco dogs, 86–87
Spices and condiments, on grocery list, 97
Spinach
   hot dog Rockefeller, 73–74
Spud pups, 42–43
   variations, 43
Stew(s)
   Irish setter, 62
   quick hot dog, 63
Stock, defined, 94
Stuffed dogs, 41–42
   variations, 42
Stuffed peppers, 66–67
   variations, 67
Stuffed potatoes, 43–44
   variations, 44
Stuffed tomatoes, 40–41
   variations, 41

Sweet potato(es)
   boats, 44–45
   yammy hot dog bake, 61–62
Sweet potato bake, 44–45
   variations, 44–45
Sweet-sour hot dogs, 56–57
   variations, 57
Swiss cheese roll-ups, 12–13
   variations, 13

Taco dogs, 86–87
   variations, 86–87
Toasted dog, French, 18
Tomato(es)
   chili dogs, 38–39
   pizza puppy toast, 39
   sloppy dog on a bun, 40
   stewed, hot dog Creole, 64–65
   stuffed, 40–41
Tossed salad, 36
   variations, 36
Totman, Mary, 51

Utensils and equipment, 3–5
   list, 99–100
   pots and pans, 100
   small things, 99–100

Vegetables, 5, 96
  cooking time for, 5, 96
  creamed corn and dogs, 48
  creamed and crispy dogs, 60–61
  divine dogs, 75
  dog pilaff, 65
  dogstick rice casserole, 66
  Down-East hot dog chowder, 30
  on grocery list, 96
  hot dog Creole, 64–65
  hot dog Florentine, 74–75
  hot dog mold, 85
  hot dog paisano, 72–73
  hot dog pie, 88–89
  hot dog Rockefeller, 73–74
  hot dogs and sauerkraut in beer, 76–77
  hot dogs Southern style, 54
  hot dog waggle, 47
  macaroni, cheese, and dogs, 50
  quick hot dog stew, 62
  sauer (green) bean hot dog casserole, 77
  savory hot dog bread pudding, 51–52
  stuffed peppers, 66–67
  sweet-sour hot dogs, 56–57
  See also specific recipes, vegetables

Wine(s)
  creamed chipped dogs, 48–49
  on grocery list, 98
  hot dog Florentine, 74–75
  potted dogs, 13

Yammy hot dog bake, 61–62
  variations, 62

Zucchini
  hot dog paisano, 72–73

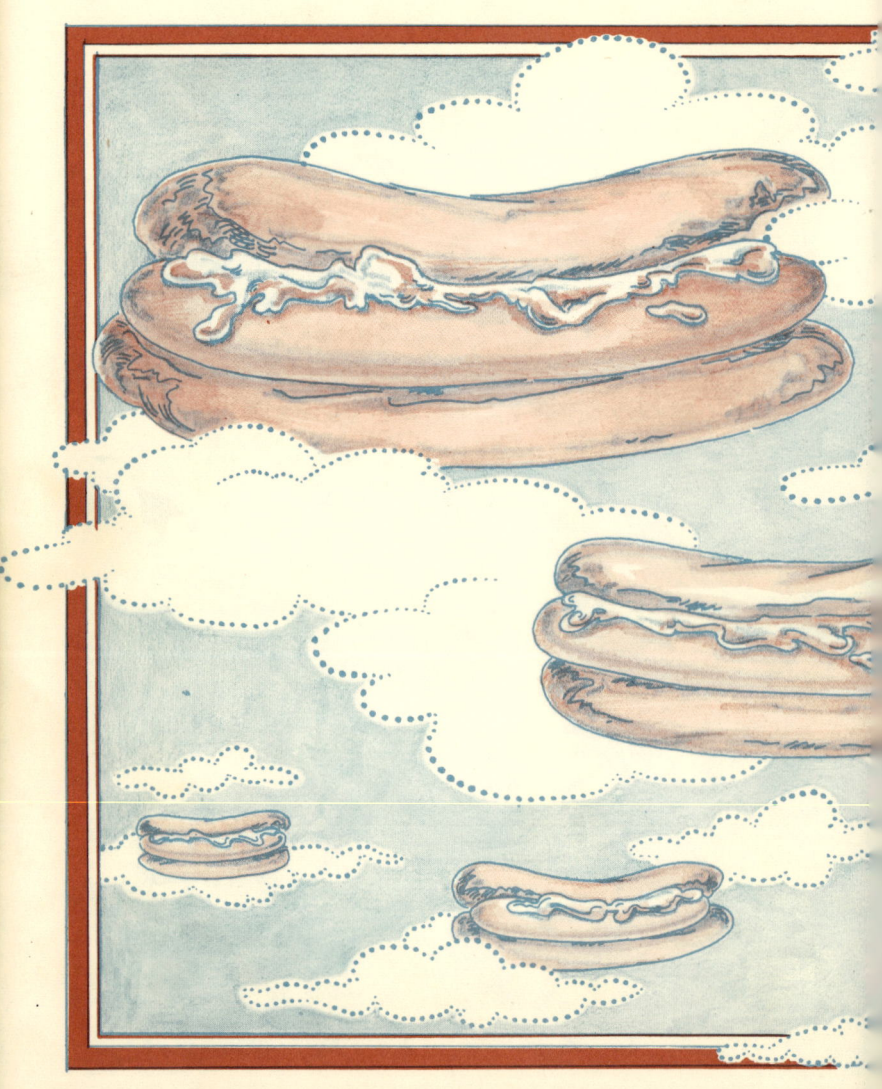